# Choose You This Day

**DICK DERKSEN**

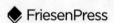 FriesenPress

Suite 300 - 990 Fort St
Victoria, BC, V8V 3K2
Canada

www.friesenpress.com

**Copyright © 2020 by Dick Derksen**
First Edition — 2020

ISBN
978-1-5255-7429-0 (Hardcover)
978-1-5255-7430-6 (Paperback)
978-1-5255-7388-0x (eBook)

*1. HISTORY, EUROPE, GERMANY*

Distributed to the trade by The Ingram Book Company

Oct. 2, 2020

Enjoy!

# The History Lesson: Prologue

This story is fictitious, but it is based in true history. The Derksens have been Mennonites throughout their known history, so this is a history of the Mennonites of northern Europe, with a somewhat mythological beginning of the Derksen clan woven into the story. Here are some important facts about the years surrounding 1556 and 1557, when our story takes place:

1. The Reformation of 1517 and onwards had many concurrent streams flowing together and separating, as strong leaders were able to influence people with their authenticity and their authority. It was preceded by groups seeking reform within the Catholic Church, such as the Brethren of the Common Life in Holland, to which Thomas a' Kempis and Erasmus of Rotterdam belonged. Groups such as the Prophets (*Propheten*) and the Enthusiasts (*Schwärmer*) at Zwickau, led by Thomas Muentzer, Melchior Hoffman and others, converged in their teachings, producing a chiliastic doctrine that demanded immediate and acute military action to bring in the Kingdom of Christ. The Peasants Revolt (1524-25) and the taking of Muenster (1534-35) were results of this movement.

2.  The Swiss Reformation under Ulrich Zwingli had another offshoot, namely the Anabaptists under Conrad Grebel, Felix Manx, George Blaurock, and others, about 1525. The Prophets and Enthusiasts from Zwickau also traveled to Zurich and fertilized the Anabaptist teachings with their particular slant on the truth. The Anabaptists fled to Strasbourg when Zwingli began persecuting them, then fled again when Martin Bucer became a Lutheran in 1534. They were influenced by Menno's teachings and took his name during the time of this book, but fled eventually to Pennsylvania, where they are today known as the "Pennsylvania Dutch." Their influence on the northern groups at this time had come through the bombastic teachings of Melchior Hoffmann, who had stopped in Strasbourg, before descending the Rhine to Holland, and out of whose ministry the Muenster debacle resulted. It was Menno's reaction against this city takeover that prompted him to convert from Catholicism to Anabaptism, so that he could counteract the bad influence of this chiliastic movement.

3.  Menno Simon was a late convert to the Anabaptist stream, in 1536, but because of his training and experience as a Catholic priest before this, and because of his personal nature, preaching and writing gifts, he soon became the recognized leader of the movement. Seeing the damage that had been done to the gospel in Muenster by Melchior Hoffman's followers, he taught nonresistance as reflecting more closely the teachings of Christ in the Sermon on the Mount.

4.  Other related groups, the Amish and the Hutterites, were finding refuge in Moravia during this time, but also landed in Canada via South Russia eventually. Another offshoot of the Anabaptist movement was the Doukabors, who originated in Russia and were Russians, who also moved to Canada eventually.

5.  The three doctrinal differences that separated the Mennists, later called Mennonites, from both the Catholic Church and the other

Protestants were 1) their refusal to recognize infant baptism as valid for salvation, 2) their rejection of the sword as a means to reach their spiritual goals, and 3) their refusal to take the oath of allegiance to the Emperor of the Holy Roman Empire, which was automatically an acceptance of the teachings of Rome.

6. The Netherlands and Flanders were particularly subject to the ideas of the Reformation, particularly Anabaptist and Calvinistic ideas, as they were under direct control of the King of Spain, who was also the Emperor of the Holy Roman Empire. Charles V was obsessed with his sense of duty to keep the power of the Church of Rome strong, because he sought to be crowned by the Pope. The Brethren of the Common Life had long taught a pietistic view of true faith, so the teachings of the Anabaptists fell on listening ears. Because there were no large cities in Friesland, there was less structure in the government, and fringe groups, such as the Anabaptists, could flourish. There were, however, violent scenes of persecution, as when the convent at Bolsward, with 300 Anabaptists seeking refuge inside, was burned to the ground by Spanish troops. Menno's brother perished in this incident, leading Menno to think about his own level of dedication to Christ.

7. On the eastern fringes of the Holy Roman Empire – thus Christian Europe – the Muslims under Suleiman the Magnificent were knocking on the doors of Vienna, after taking Buda and Pest. The Balkans had already fallen to their rule. Soldiers were conscripted from every prince in the Empire by the new Emperor, Ferdinand of Austria, the brother of Charles V, to fight off the Turks from Vienna, which provided a door into the rest of Christian Europe.

8. Led by his predecessors, Obbe and Dirk Philips, Menno taught that true Christians act and dress differently from the world. During his many years of leadership, this was re-assessed frequently, but was generally maintained by all groups. Rites such as foot-washing and the use of the ban for those who refused the discipline of the elders

were practiced with varying rigor, but it was sometimes these practices that separated one strong leader from another, causing rifts within the Mennonite Church.

9. The Peace of Augsburg, 25 September 1555, allowed each prince in the Holy Roman Empire to choose the religion of his domain (*cuius regio, eius religio*), without further threat of invasion by imperial troops. Nothing is said about conversions from one religion to another within the realm, but it was assumed that all subjects would follow the religious choice of their prince.

10. Bartholomew von Ahlefeld, of whom little is known personally, commanded a battalion in Holland's War of Independence from Spanish dominion in 1542. He may have visited Flanders during this time. He noticed that Anabaptists were a peaceful, law-abiding people with great skills, which he thought was a commendable combination for his own estates. As a "minor nobleman," he inherited the Fresenburg Estate soon after his military career. This included Bad Oldesloe and its surrounding villages, such as Wuestenfelde, and from 1543 onwards he invited oppressed Mennists to settle on his estates. Since he is only referred to as a "minor nobleman," I have chosen to call him a Baron, subject under serfdom to Duke Adolf of Holstein-Gottorp. Although Duke Adolf of Holstein-Gottorp, an ardent Lutheran in league with his brother, King Christian III of Denmark, sought to dissuade von Ahlefeld from protecting this hated sect, he and those who followed him persisted until 1627-29, when Danish Lutheran troops sacked Wuestenfelde in the Thirty Years War. There is no record of his having converted, but he admired the Mennonites, a name they began to take during the time that Menno resided on his estate. Because he appeared to have progressive views, von Ahlefeld has been cast as a rich, wide-thinking man with good connections among the nobility, who meant well in protecting those

who were persecuted for their religion, but remained, at least out-wardly, a Catholic.

11. Menno brought a printer and printing press with him, to continue his publishing of books and tracts, and von Ahlefeld allowed him to do so. The Menno Kate (Kah-teh = Cottage) was used for this. The Menno Linde is a tree reportedly planted by Menno. There are various monuments to Menno's time in Bad Oldesloe and Wuestenfelde. We know that Menno used crutches in his later years, but he continued to travel to Mennonite congrega-tions throughout northern Europe, and possibly as far south as Strasbourg. Pictures painted of him are all of a much later date, so they are artists' conceptions, taken from eyewitness accounts, of what he might have looked like. They depict him with a full beard and a round, kindly face. His dates of birth and death are disputed. His birth is believed to have been around 1492, and his death was likely in January, 1559, a couple of years after this story takes place. I took the liberty to place it during the time of this volume, to keep the cohesiveness of the story line.

12. Anabaptists from Flanders fled to Friesland, where they met with others of like mind, who were being led by Menno, and joined his group. They brought a new form of strictness to church govern-ment, perhaps more necessary in the large commercial centers of Flanders than in the pastoral countryside of Friesland. Many of the Friesian Anabaptists took on the strict Flemish view. This has created difficulty in tracing the name Derksen, as families with this name were listed in Prussia as Flemish, but that information was taken from their church affiliation, rather than their geographic origin. The name is clearly Friesian, meaning "belonging to Derks." This can be seen when a Mennonite calls himself "Derksen Dick" instead of Dick Derksen – the "en" ending denoting an adjectival form of the word Derks. The idea that "sen" denotes "son of," as in

Scandinavian names, apparently does not agree with the etymology of the Dutch names.

13. Various epidemics decimated Europe during the 16th and 17th Centuries, one of them being influenza. Others were typhus, diphtheria, measles, smallpox and the Black Plague. Influenza was common, unknown of origin, quite selective and often fatal, much as the COVID-19 virus of our time.

14. Stoves as we know them were basically unknown in the 16th Century. The fireplace and spit, along with a boom to hang a pot, were pretty much what was available. Bread and pastries were usually baked in a communal oven in each village, as the making of such ovens entailed great skilled labor and selected materials. Derksens have always been inventive, so Jacob Derksen has been cast as one who had learned to build stoves and ovens as a bricklayer in projects involving rich noblemen, and thus he built one for his family, and then in others of his building projects.

15. Food during the late Middle Ages was different from today's fare. The New World had just been discovered, and explorers were bringing new products to Spain and Portugal, some of which became standard fare a century later. Only the nobility could afford such luxuries at this time. Most people ate a soup or stew of vegetables and grain, sometimes with a bit of meat, along with course bread, for their main meals. The "traditional" Mennonite dishes, which many will be searching for in this book, actually came later, though a limited few that were possible at the time have been introduced. Potatoes, corn, squash, and beans (other than fava beans) are just some that came from the New World. Spices, such as pepper and cinnamon, came as the result of new explorations in Southeastern Asia at this time, made possible by the discovery of a route around the Cape of Good Hope in South Africa, by Bartholomew Diaz and Vasco da Gama, of Portugal. Because of the forward-thinking

Bartholomew von Ahlefeld, a couple of these are introduced into the story.

16. Transportation in the 16th Century was basically by horseback or by horse and wagon, or pedestrian. Fancy buggies and carriages were only coming in for the nobility at the time. Walking was the most common mode of transportation, thus people generally didn't go far from their homes. The three kilometers between Wuestenfelde and Bad Oldesloe would have been quite an acceptable walking distance for the peasants.

17. Education was becoming more and more available, having come under widespread interest in the Renaissance in the previous century. Much of it was promoted through church-sponsored schools and universities that had recently come into being. Mennonites believed that education would turn their children against their simple faith. Therefore, only a minimum of schooling was permitted. This consisted mainly of rudimentary reading, writing and arithmetic, with a generous dose of Bible memorization and Dutch hymns.

18. I should say a word about my spellings of terms in Plautdietsch: In general, I have adopted the equivalent High German spelling for the sounds of the dialect. That is contrary to how many 'Russian Mennonites' in Canada and USA spell their writings, where an Anglicized spelling is preferred. Because I lived in Germany for so long, my High German is much better than my Plautdietsch, so I drift naturally into how the Germans would spell their dialect terms. I have avoided the use of the Umlaut, which is two dots above the letter, as it presents printing problems, as well as reading problems for those not introduced to its use. Instead I have substituted, as Germans also do, the vowel plus an 'e' to indicate where the vowel would normally have an Umlaut. The function of the Umlaut is to change the pronunciation of the vowel. The reader will also note that in German, all nouns are capitalized, except

adjectival nouns. German vowels are normally straight, that is, they follow what we in the choral world call 'Italian vowels', where we sing ah, ay, ee, oh, uh, instead of the English ay, ee, eye, oh, you. When these sounds differ from the open vowel, the Umlaut is used to indicate that change of sound, so the ah (letter "a" in English) sound diverts to ae, which is pronounced like the ai in 'said', but with the lips pulled inwards from the sides. The Umlaut is used primarily with a, o and u, which in my text renders them ae, oe and ue. Another Germanism is the fact that ei is pronounced like 'eye' in English, while ie is pronounced like 'ee'. Consonants, such as W and J also have different pronunciations from the English equivalents. "W" is pronounced as a V would be in English, and "J" is pronounced as Y in the word you.

My plan is to write other volumes in this family history, incorporating the historical wanderings of my Mennonite ancestors, and the issues that molded their lives and beliefs. Since the Derksens can be traced back as having participated in a number of stages in these wanderings, I projected the story backwards ultimately to the time of Menno Simon in Holland, but centered it in Bad Oldesloe and Wuestenfelde, where they might have settled along with Menno. This extended story combines the fruits of years of reading in all thes areas. It is my wish that the reader absorb the geographical and historical settings, so that the story itself can take shape within them, and that allowance will be made for creativity in the story details. My purpose in writing this book is not to make it read like a history book, though the history is as accurate as I can make it. I have, therefore, not listed a bibliography of books and sources I have consulted, nor have I generated an index. Both would have been useful to some who wish to study further, but can be gotten elsewhere.

I have noticed that some Mennonites, even in the Derksen clan, have "latched onto" certain stories in our history, claiming them to be true, when their veracity may well be challenged by other researchers, so I realize that I may have "latched onto" a different aspect of the story than they have.

As a youth I grew up in a pioneering situation near Vanderhoof, British Columbie, as the oldest of fifteen children. I was unable to attend high school, as I entered the work force in my father's sawmill, and also learned carpentry and mechanics from him, as well as farming, before entering Bible school at twenty years of age. I then completed ten years of schooling to become a teacher. I am an historian, a Bible and church history teacher, as well as a school music teacher by profession, with doctoral-level education in the philosophy of Christian education, which I did just before I retired in 2007.

I apologize, if I have missed something important in my reading of history. I lived for 31 years in the Black Forest and Austria, working in schools for missionary children. I have visited Witmarsum, but not Bad Oldesloe, though I have been near it. Enjoy and be blessed, as I have enjoyed and been blessed in researching and writing this book.

The next volume will trace the first movement of the group from Wuestenfelde to Altona, just outside Hamburg, Germany, during the Thirty Years War. Naturally, it will be a later generation that comes into play here, but I will continue to give the main character the name of Jacob Derksen, for it was Dr. Jacob Derksen who brought the Derksens to Canada. Subsequent volumes will center in West Prussia, in South Russia, and eventually, in Canada, with historical details from the respective places and times incorporated into the story. Enjoy Mennonite history in a new format.

# Geneology of the Derksen Family

## As created by Dick Derksen, November, 2010, and April, 2020

| Jacob | Age | Places Lived | Details | Children | Occupation |
|---|---|---|---|---|---|
| Jacob Derksen I | 1505-1580 | Witmarsum, various, Muenster, Witmarsum, Wuestenfelde | Converted to Mennism over a period of time around 1536, along with Menno Simon. Married to Eva; eight children, of whom 5 survive to adulthood. | Henry<br>Leah<br>Jake<br>Aron<br>Frederic<br>Isaac<br>Sarah<br>Miriam (Schaetzli) | Mason, Deacon in Mennonite Church, Built barns for Baron Bartholomew von Ahlefeld |
| Jacob II (Jake) | 1536-1627 | Wuestenfelde, Bad Oldesloe, Altona | With the martyrdom of Henry, Jake becomes the oldest male, second to Leah, who is a year older. Jake marries Heidi, has one son, Jacob III. | | Carpentry in the Baron's shop, deacon in Mennonite Church |

| Jacob III | 1581-1650 | Wuestenfleide, Altona | | | |
|---|---|---|---|---|---|
| | | | Born after years of barrenness, married to Rebekah Thiessen, by whom five children are born. Rebekah dies in delivery of Jacob IV (JJ). | Benjamin → Joshua, Mary, Elizabeth, Jacob IV | Carpentry in the Baron's shop; preacher in Mennonite Church, Manager of Mennonite Manufacturing (wagons, ironware) Elder in the Mennonite district |
| | | | They take in five Guenther children, whose parents die of the Plague. Marries the widow Martina Roosen, but the unconsummated marriage is annulled; | Guenther Children: Susan, Nickolas, Jonathan →, Agnes, Willy | |
| | | | then he marries his cousin Dorcas, daughter of Leah and Heinrich Gerbrandt. | Roosen Children: Gerritt, Lizzy → | |
| | | | Five children with Rebekah, two with Dorcas; sort of adopted the two Roosen children. Planning to move to Heubuden, Royal Prussia, but thwarted. | Children by Dorcas → Heinrich Jacob, Heidi Leah | |

| | | | Mennonite | Manufacturing | Farmer |
|---|---|---|---|---|---|
| Jacob IV (JJ) | 1628-1685 | Altona | | | Lives his entire life in Altona, carrying on his father's business, but branching out into farming. Marries, has twelve children, with Jacob V (JD) as youngest male. |
| Jacob V (JD) | 1675-1758 | Altona, Heubuden | | Farmer | Although his father dies when he is but ten, he thrives under the tutelage of his older brothers and his devoted mother. In 1704 he and his older brothers move to West Prussia with their families and set up farming in the marshlands of the Vistula Delta. Prussian rule brings both good and bad things into the lives of the Mennonites. Has ten children, of which Jacob VI is the middle son. |

| | | | | | |
|---|---|---|---|---|---|
| Jacob VI | 1700-1790 | Heubuden | Lives his entire life in Heubuden, farming and running the windmill pump that drains the land. Jacob VII is his youngest son, born of his second wife. Volume III is based in this time and is set in Heubuden, Royal Prussia. He does not go to South Russia, but dies shortly after the Great Trek. | | Farmer<br>Derksen<br>Sugar Refining |
| Jacob VII | 1742-1818 | Heubuden, Chortiza | During his time the Mennonites emigrated to Chortiza, along the Dnieper River in South Russia, just above the Black Sea. | Daniel-Suzie<br>Bertha-Henry<br>Kate-John<br>Joseph-Emily<br>Anna<br>Jacob VIII<br>Thomas<br>Wilhelm | Farmer<br>Derksen<br>Sugar Refining |

| | | | | | Derksen |
|---|---|---|---|---|---|
| Jacob VIII | 1770-1850 | Heubuden, Chortiza | He is the earliest ancestor whose date of birth is known. He was born in Heubuden, Royal Prussia. His wife's name was Katrina Peters, also born in Heubuden. They had four children, beginning eight years after their marriage. Volume IV is set in this time. | Maria 1798 Jacob IX 1804 Anna 1805 Helma Helena 1808 | Sugar Refinery Farmer |
| Jacob IX | 1804-1879 | Chortiza, Bergthal, Steinbach, Gretna | This is Dr. Jacob Derksen, who, though his wife, Sara Giesbrecht, died in 1873, brought the clan over from South Russia to Manitoba in 1874, settling first in East Reserve and then in the West Reserve, near Gretna. | | Farmer Veterinarian Medical Doctor |

| Name | Dates | Locations | Notes | Occupation |
| --- | --- | --- | --- | --- |
| Heinrich I | 1844-1913 | Bergthal, Steinbach, Gretna | In this generation my ancestry departs from the Jacobs and moves to the Henry's, known in German as Heinrich. He was a prosperous farmer, who gave each of his children 80 acres, a cow, horses, chickens and geese on their marriage. Of thirteen children, six died in infancy, two on the trip to Canada and four through a flu epidemic. | Farmer |
| Heinrich II (HG) | 1880-1964 | Gretna, Lowe Farm, Mission, BC, Winnipeg, MB | Born in Canada, the third son to be named Heinrich, as the first two died in infancy. Moved away from the rest of the family to settle in Lowe Farm. Eleven children, of whom Henry III is my father. | Farmer |

| Name | Dates | Places | Description | Occupations |
|---|---|---|---|---|
| Henry III (HH) | 1913-1974 | Lowe Farm, Mission, Vanderhoof | Moving from farm to carpentry, then to sawmilling and bush farming, finally to working in a store, he raised fifteen children, of whom the author is the eldest. | Prairie Farmer<br>Carpenter<br>Mechanic/Welder<br>Sawmill Operator<br>Bush Farmer |
| Richard John (Dick) | 1939- | Lowe Farm, Mission, Vanderhoof, Three Hills, Calgary, Kandern, Vienna, Kandern, Calgary | Eldest of fifteen children, of whom two sets were twins. Worked in his father's sawmill until almost 21, and then went to Prairie Bible Institute for four years, graduating in 1964, after which he finished high school there, having only completed Grade IX by correspondence in a bush camp. He graduated from Prairie High School in 1966. Married Jeraldine Wilkinson August 31, 1968, in the middle of his B.Ed. Finishing university in 1970, he taught in Calgary for six years and directed Whispering Pines Bible Camp and had two sons, | School Teacher/<br>Band Director<br>Camp Director<br>Missionary Teacher/<br>Administrator<br>Music Arranger/<br>Composer<br>Author |

Derek (1971) and Devon (1973), then went to Kandern, Germany, to Black Forest Academy (1976), with Janz Team Ministries. He was loaned out to begin Vienna Christian School in 1986 and returned to BFA in 1991, after the school was well established. He served as Academic Dean until 2007. His wife and he are presently retired in Calgary. Although he was raised in the Menno-nite tradition, he never joined a Men-nonite church; his church member-ships have been in Associated Gospel, Evangelical Free and Baptist churches. He cher-ishes the Mennonite traditions, espe-cially those involving food.

Volume V is set in this time, with flashbacks to the move from Russia to Canada, and the various generations that intervened.

# Chapter One

Christmas Eve, 1556, in Wuestenfelde, a small village near Bad Oldesloe, between Hamburg and Lübeck, in northern Germany, was peaceful and filled with joy for the Derksen family. Jacob and Eva, with their children around them, sat in the large family room of their house, basking in the warmth of the wood-burning hearth against one wall of their home, which was built in the typical wooden frame construction, daubed with a mixture of clay and straw, with a thatched roof of reeds from the nearby swamp, that was common among peasant families throughout northern Europe in the Sixteenth Century.

Their supper simmered in the cast iron pots that hung from a special crane over the open fire. Jacob Derksen had used his bricklaying experience to fashion a cast iron surface that formed another cooking area with an extension of the fire pit underneath, and some things were in smaller pots on that surface. He had also seen an oven built into the chimney above the open hearth on one of his jobs in a lordly mansion, and in his resourcefulness had incorporated this innovation into their new home. The home was not large for a family with eight children, some of whom were young adults, but it was cozy and comfortable, as the wind whipped snow in swirls and eddies around every corner of

19

their farmyard. There were no decorations to mark this joyous season, only the rosy, healthy glow of happy faces sharing in the familiar presence of each other.

"Will we open our presents tonight, Father?" asked Miriam, the youngest.

"Maybe there won't be any presents, Schaetzli," teased Jacob.

"There will be, I saw the bundles in the bench under your bed," retorted four-year-old Miriam, known in the family by her nickname, Schaetzli, which meant "little treasure" in German.

"You weren't supposed to be looking, Schaetzli," returned her father reproachfully, "You know that this is the time of year when we keep secrets and things are hidden from one another, so that we can surprise each other."

"Oh, I can't wait any longer," snapped the little treasure, pouting.

"Well, we won't be opening any bundles until we have had our supper and cleaned up the dishes," Eva, the mother, announced loudly from her position by the stove, and that was final. Miriam went over to her older sister, Leah, for comfort.

"And we will tell the precious Christmas story, too, before we open anything." announced Jacob, almost as loudly. "Is supper ready, Eva? I'm starving." There were nods of approval and sighs of anticipation all around.

At this there was general movement toward the table, with its corner bench, a short part along one end of the table, and a long part that extended down the long side of the table, with a free-standing bench along the other long side of the table, and handmade chairs on the end for the parents. The youngest children scampered to their places near mother and father, and the older ones lined up according to age further down the table, with Henry, the oldest one at 22, at the far end. Mother sat between Jacob and Miriam, in case she needed to help her.

All heads were bowed in silent prayer, which somehow finished for everyone at the same time, and the food began its rounds, with all helping themselves to that which was nearest on the table and passing it to one who was ready to receive it. Large families had learned how an efficient table was set and served with minimal delay and effort, and the Derksens were efficient to the letter. There was little conversation as they began to sample the food, except for a squabble that broke out between two of the younger brothers about a piece of goose that each wanted. Jacob glared at them, and Aron grudgingly gave the piece to Frederic. Again, this was part of the efficiency that marked their family; there was no real need for father to speak; the boys knew exactly what he meant and what would happen to them if they didn't obey the silent command.

"Isn't it wonderful of our Baron to provide us with such a delightful Christmas Eve dinner?" ventured Mother tentatively, to ease the tenseness of the situation. She looked around at her husband and the other children with a hopeful, beaming radiance.

Although the goose they were eating came from their own farm, everything else they needed for their Christmas Eve supper had been provided by Baron Bartholomew von Ahlefeld, on whose property they were living, and for whom they were farming their plot. Because of the religious persecutions that had followed them, the Derksens had moved about a great deal, so they were deeply thankful for the relative peace and security of their new home. This had been their second crop in Wuestenfelde, and their labors had been amply rewarded with a good return from both field and garden, for which the good Baron had supplied the implements and the seed. Being a progressive nobleman, the Baron had introduced seedlings from South America that had recently been brought by the explorers to Europe, and Jacob and Eva had been rewarded with a good crop of potatoes, which they were now seeking to preserve from the winter cold. Their cow had borne twin heifers and was producing lots of milk, and the sow had borne a litter of eight piglets that were now fattening up to supply meat for the next year and breeding stock to begin a family hog operation. Chickens were laying well, and geese and ducks were also doing well. God had indeed been very good to their family, and Mother was deeply thankful for His rich blessings. The village dogs barked and fought outside in the cold, or snuggled into warmer nooks and crannies around the barns, while the cats prowled around the barn, looking for delicious and unwary rodents that might be scurrying about in the dark.

It was some time before Father took his sharp eyes off the offending sons, but then he responded with a great sigh. "Yes, God has indeed been good to us." Jacob was mindful more of the Almighty's bountiful hand than he was of the good nobleman's largesse. It had been a hard twenty-two years since he and his wife had converted to the new religion of the Anabaptists. Persecution came from both sides, and fleeing was the only way to preserve what little of life was left to them. Jacob glanced at Eva admiringly, for she had been a stalwart warrior for the faith. With her feet firmly on the ground for her family, her mind was in the heavenlies, just as his was.

But now they must celebrate. The last pieces of the goose carcass were being picked over for any morsel of meat or gristle that could be relieved of its tasty treasure, and the gravy bowl was being wiped clean with a piece of Leah's homemade bread. That is, it was Leah's first attempt at baking Bulki, the white wheat bread that their family loved so much, and Mother had kept a watchful eye over the initial efforts of her eldest daughter, now 21 years old. A mother must train her daughters to be good wives and mothers, and Eva was not going to fail in this important responsibility. *My, where has the time gone, that my children are now grown up?* she wondered.

Tomorrow they would be feasting on Tweiback, the interesting little double rolls that had more crusty area than the Einback, which were singular buns, but also had the soft area between the two parts of the bun that were squeezed together. For tonight, though, the Bulki was just right, for it was better for sopping up leftover gravy. Leah smiled proudly as she saw her workmanship fulfilling its destiny in the hands of her younger brothers.

Henry, who was a year older than Leah, and Jake, who was a year younger, sat on each side of her at the table. Neither had said anything, but both had been thoroughly absorbed in their enjoyment of the meal. Both were finishing up with a slice of <u>Bulki</u> with butter, which was a special treat for this meal. Because their cow produced lots of rich milk, there was a goodly amount of cream left for churning. In this regard the family was become less limited in its resources, for they now had several milk cows. The other Anabaptist families that had immigrated to the Fresenburg estate were also large, and they also felt extremely grateful for the one milk cow that they had each received from the Baron on their arrival on the estate.

Since the Derksens' origin was in the Lowlands, in Friesland in northwestern Netherlands, their Low German dialect was similar to that of those in northern Germany. Communication, therefore, was not a problem, though some terms were more German and others more Dutch in the common dialect. The grammar was thus simplified, and this language would become part of the basis of Middle English eventually. In their church services, these distinctions were beginning to be heard, as the messages were often written out by one minister and read by others in the area, thus standardizing the dialect on a wider scale. Unlike the Derksens and others among the Anabaptists, the ministers were educated and could read the local cultured language and also Latin, as well as the local dialect insofar as it was written down. A minimal elementary education was all that Jacob and Eva could boast, and their children were not receiving more. Schools were where the worldly ideas of the wicked people around them, both Catholics and Lutherans, were picked up by the children, so to protect the children from such worldly influence, the parents only allowed them to attend school until they had a basic grasp of reading, writing and arithmetic.

Isaac, five years younger than Jacob, but older than Sarah, chewed contemplatively on a final morsel of gristle from the goose carcass. Although he looked quite healthy and strong, as his fifteen-year-old body had entered adolescence, his mind did not develop as the others, and he occasionally acted inappropriately in social situations. He had not said or done anything inappropriate tonight, for which all were thankful. Sarah, on the other hand, was bright, lively and very much an eleven-year-old girl. Her blond braids bounced as her head danced to an inner melody, and she stared in wonder at the bare bones and empty serving bowls before her in the center of the table and rubbed her greasy hands on her dress. She relished the fact that school was out for the holidays, and she could enjoy her family and friends in the village.

Father announced sternly that they would now recite the Christmas story, and then looked around to make sure that everyone was paying close attention. Everyone was, as was normal when Father was about to lead in family worship. With obvious joy and conviction, he began to tell the story of Jesus' birth in the manger in Bethlehem, the angels' chorus, the shepherds' visit, and Mary and Joseph's care for the baby Savior, and ending with the visit of the Magi and the flight into Egypt. As it has through the ages, the story thrilled the hearts of parents, young people and children alike with its simplicity and depth of meaning. Hearing it made it seem as though it might have happened in their very own house-barn. Following the telling of the Christmas story, Father asked whether anyone had a suggestion for a song that they might sing together. No one could think of one that they knew the words for, until Mother began humming a song that all recognized. Soon all began remembering lines from the various verses. With no books or Bibles available, worship tended to be a time of recall of things that had been learned in school or in church.

"Now can we open our presents?" Miriam's plaintive plea, muffled by her mother's sleeve, in which she had buried her face in a fanciful thought, pierced everyone's heart with sympathetic resonance. The wait had taken its toll on Schaetzli's attention span, and she was ready for the long-awaited action. Sarah, Aron and Frederic joined vociferously in the chorus of anticipation, while Isaac was absorbed in his own world of fantasy.

At that, Father left the room and went next door into the parental bedroom and dug around in the box underneath the bench-like construction that made up their bed frame. These pieces of furniture were built to do three things – to become the platform for the mattress of straw and down, to store the bedding during daytimes, and to act as a bench for sitting on when not extended out to be the bed for the night. Most of the gifts had been hidden underneath the straw and feather tick at the bottom of the storage box under the bench, to keep them from investigative eyes and hands.

The same arrangement could be seen in every room, where a similar bench-bed graced one wall, a wardrobe stood against another, and a chest of drawers against the third. Even the family room had one such double bench-bed plus a smaller couch, and this is where the girls slept. In the attic, under the thatch, was where the boys had their straw ticks, carefully protected from insects, mice and rats that sometimes infested the thatch.

On the chest in Father and Mother's room stood a basin and a pitcher, to be used for washing up. Towels were hung over a bar arrangement near the part of the brick chimney that protruded into their room, thus giving a form of central heating to the whole house. In that way the towels were always dry for the next usage, and in this weather, even somewhat warm. Beside the towel were stockings and pants that had gotten wet while the chores were being done.

Father called for Henry and Jacob Jr to come and help bring out some of the bundles, as some were larger than others, and some had clumsy protrusions. In the meantime, Mother and the older girls cleared the table and decked it with a fresh cloth to receive the bundles from the other room. Together the men brought armfuls of bundles into the family room and placed them on the tablecloth. There were ten bundles, one for each person in the room. From the appearance of the wrappings, it would seem that all of the presents were from the Baron, who had generously provided all that Jacob and his Anabaptist friends would need for their families.

Mother was called upon to distribute each bundle to the right person. Sarah was commissioned to fold and put away the wrapping paper, so that no mess would be made. The first gift went to Miriam, whose patience was wearing quite thin. Everyone watched as she opened it, her four-year-old hands not sparing any paper for Sarah to fold or to save. That would serve to help light the fire, should it ever be left to go out. Out of the torn wrappings came a lovely rag doll, with a bright dress and bonnet, and rosy patches of cloth on the cheeks. She immediately left the table to begin carrying it like a baby, swaying from side to side as she hugged her new treasure, and singing childish songs to it in her happiness. Sarah was next, and hers was a brush set for her hair. As soon as she had folded the paper, she let out her braids and began fiercely to brush her blond hair, which fell to the middle of her back. Frederic was very pleased with his warm new overcoat, which he donned with obvious pleasure and Aron with his wagon, which Jacob Jr helped him put together. For Isaac there was a small wheelbarrow, which Henry assembled for him from the pieces in the package. Jacob lovingly caressed his new German Bible, which he would delight in reading, as soon as his reading of that language improved sufficiently. Leah received a new long dress, soft grey with blue trim, not too fancy to alert her mother to possible dangers, and not too plain to make it unacceptable for a girl in young womanhood. For Henry there was a new pair of boots, just what he needed for his hard work in the carpentry shop. Mother received a nice dress and Father a new suit, which he could use for his duties at their church. The pile of neatly-folded wrapping paper was then carefully bound with string and carried into Mother and Father's room, where all precious items were kept.

"Father, tell us how we got to live here in Wuestenfelde," came a chorus from the younger ones. As the table was once more cleared of all that remained from the unwrapping of the gifts, Mother took this as a signal to begin puttering in the kitchen part of the great family room. A large pan of Perischki, or fruit pockets, appeared as if from nowhere, and hot mulled wine in a pot on the back of the stove was checked for temperature, and cups were distributed around the table. The pan of desserts took center stage in the middle of the table and the cups were each filled with the pungent liquid.

"To our health," said Father, lifting his cup. "To our health," repeated the rest of the family in unison, and then they all took a draft of the sweet, warm drink. How good it was on such a cold and blustery evening to have a drink that seemed to penetrate the soul as it settled into the body. The <u>Perischki</u> disappeared immediately into twenty eager hands, and amid satisfied grunts and longer aspirations, the family settled down to hear what Father would say.

# Chapter Two

Father sipped slowly and deeply from his cup and began: "Mother and I grew up in Witmarsum, Netherlands, where we went to school, were part of the local Catholic Church, and where we got married. As we were growing up, we became aware of unrest in the church. Some were listening to the calls for a deeper inner spiritual life, as preached by the Brethren of the Common Life, a Catholic order that emphasized pietistic religion as an expression of the soul, rather than of the outward liturgy of the church. Some read the devotional studies of Thomas à Kempis, who had been one of the leading figures in the Brethren movement a century before. Erasmus, who was also a member of the Brethren, shocked the Catholic world by introducing a Latin New Testament translated out of the original Greek, instead of being based on the Catholic Vulgate, the Latin Bible used by the church. We began to attend meetings of the Brethren in Witmarsum and were moved by their genuineness of faith and life.

"Then we had a visitor from Strasbourg, a member of a new sect being called Anabaptists by the church. His name was Melchior Hoffmann, and he had come originally from Zwickau in eastern Germany, where he was one of the Prophets and he had been influenced by the Enthusiasts. The first group believed that the world was soon coming to an end and studied the Bible for clues to the date and time of this cataclysm. The second group practiced a pietistic enthusiasm in their worship that came from deep within. Hoffmann, though we found out that he had been chased out of Strasbourg later by the other Anabaptists for being a pest with his strange beliefs and bombastic preaching, really got the people out for his meetings. These were held in machine sheds and barns, to avoid detection by church officials. We went, too, and we were moved by what he said. More and more, we became convinced that the Anabaptist belief in baptism of believers only was better than the baptism of babies, as the church practiced. We were baptized in one of the meetings.

"We followed the teachings of Hoffmann and then his followers, but we also attended the local Catholic Church to avoid being persecuted. We even got married in the church, to avoid looking like we were not faithful. Sometimes it was difficult to live this double life, but many were doing so, and we took comfort in that.

"Jan Mattijs of Haarlem and Jan van Leyden, who were followers of Hoffmann, but who thought the Kingdom of God should be set up on earth immediately, in preparation for Christ's Second Coming, seized Muenster, in northeastern Germany, expelled the Lutheran leadership and the Catholics, and set up the Davidic Kingdom under their leadership. We decided that we would move to Muenster and be part of the Kingdom. We packed our few belongings and found a cart going that direction, on which we could transport our few things and ourselves to Muenster. Henry was born just after we got to Muenster.

"I took work with a bricklayer, and soon we were comfortably settled in one of the apartments that had been vacated by expelled Catholics. Meanwhile, the leaders of the Kingdom seemed to hear voices telling them to re-enact scenes from the Old Testament. Bishop Franz of Waldeck, the ruler of the territory, had begun the siege of the city. Jan Mattijs took a few men outside the city and attempted to annihilate the enemy troops with God's power, but was killed in the process.

Jan van Leyden took over, but he introduced polygamy into the city. Hille Feicken sacrificed herself in an attempt to kill the bishop, using the model of Judith, who beheaded Holofernes in Israel. She was captured and put to death. All this bravado in the name of the Anabaptists shook our faith quite a bit, and many of our friends left the Anabaptists over this incident, but we decided that there was deeper truth to these beliefs than these people saw, so we stayed in the faith.

"We knew that we must escape, so we packed up again and sneaked out of the city in a wagon hauling trash to a place outside the city. From there we didn't really know where to go, but God seemed to direct us to safe houses, where we were allowed to stay until we could go further. We decided to go back to Witmarsum, where I again took up bricklaying and we moved into a house that was empty. Leah was born there. We met the priest from Pingjum, Menno Simon, who had also grown up in Witmarsum. He had moved back from Pingjum, the next village, to become the priest in Witmarsum. After hearing of the beheading of Sicke Freerks Snijder at Leeuwarden for being "re-baptized," Menno Simon became interested in a faith that would command such dedication. When his own brother, Pieter, was executed for his Anabaptist faith, when the convent in Bolsward, in which he and 300 Anabaptists had hidden, was burned to the ground with all of them in it, Menno began searching his own heart and found he also believed as this heretical group did and began attending some of their secret meetings. He gave up his priesthood and was baptized by the Anabaptists, and began preaching in the secret meetings in sheds and barns around the area. This was the spring of 1536. We hung on every word, for he made sense out of the chaos that we felt inside, with our feelings going three ways at once – to the Catholic Church, the Lutheran Protestants, and the Anabaptists.

"We learned from Menno that the Catholic Church teachings were not based on biblical truth, but were simply based in traditions of man. Martin Luther had also challenged that, Menno said. But we saw that Luther's reforms did little to change people's lives. It seemed more of a political and economic movement to us, with little else to show for it in the lives of those who became Lutherans. The revolt in Muenster had been quelled by the Emperor and the Bishop's troops, and all the leaders of the New Kingdom of David had been executed. The city and the church were now firmly back in imperial and church power, therefore, Catholic.

"Menno (He was usually called by his first name only.) culled out all the false theology, it seemed to us, and left us with a better foundation of belief. He preached nonresistance instead of war as being more in line with Christ's teaching in the Sermon on the Mount to 'Love your enemies and pray for those who persecute you.' The Bible also taught that we should not swear oaths. And we should not wear fancy clothing, as the world around does, to make an impression on people around us. We liked that teaching, because it made sense to us as the best expression of what Christ wanted His followers to live like before the world. (Leah, who had not entered wholeheartedly into her parents' strict way of life, was not impressed with this part of Menno's teachings, and allowed her mouth to form a pout.)

"It was hard to keep up a front with the Catholic Church and also follow our beliefs. We wanted to keep Henry from having to be baptized in the church, but that seemed to be impossible. We convinced ourselves that it was really just a dedication of ourselves to raise him into the true Christian faith, so that he could make his own decision later, and we had him baptized as a Catholic. That kept the persecutors away from our door, but it didn't keep our consciences from talking back to us.

"Henry nodded, for he had recently submitted to adult baptism under Menno's teachings, having confessed his personal faith in Christ alone for his salvation.

Father continued, "Menno couldn't stay in Witmarsum; both the church and the local magistrates were looking for him as a heretic. Although many people hid him at various times, it became too dangerous for him to stay. By October of 1536 his connection with Anabaptism was well-known. In that month Herman and Gerrit Jansz were arrested and charged with having lodged him. Menno was married to Gertrude shortly following his time in Witmarsum. For many years he lived as a fugitive, for a while in Emden, for a while in Cologne, and then in Wismar, always avoiding the clutches of the church and of the imperial troops that worked together with the church to stamp out what they saw as heresy. Charles V felt that it was his duty as Emperor of the Holy Roman Empire to stamp out anything that challenged his strong faith in the religion that propped up his claim to power over most of Europe.

"We became fugitives along with Menno, living where we could avoid detection. Sometimes we were in Holland, other times we were in Germany, but always on the watch for efforts to stamp out Anabaptism and its followers. We heard from others that some Anabaptists had even gone north into Denmark to avoid detection. Bricklaying continued to be my job, whenever I could get work. I guess somewhere in there we made up our minds that we believed the Anabaptist teachings and not those of the church and were ready to pay the price. All you other children were born in different places along the way.

"Finally we heard of Baron Bartholomew von Ahlefeld, who had led a Dutch uprising against the Emperor in 1542, and then had inherited this huge estate, Fresenburg, in 1543, where he invited Anabaptists to come and settle down in peace. Previous settlers had probably died of the plague or some other pestilence, so whole villages on the estate were not settled any more. That left already-built houses for us, some were even furnished, but empty. We followed other Anabaptists here. Our first two years here have been very difficult, as we were all trying to get settled, while attending to the Baron's fields and livestock. He has been most gracious to us all, and everything we have today, we have because of his generosity. Apparently some Anabaptists he met in Flanders had made quite an impression on him for their honesty and quiet lives of hard work and avoidance of trouble, so he has taken our side against the Catholic and imperial system. He, like we tried at the beginning, hasn't left the church, but openly criticizes it and the imperial system

33

it generates. Although Adolf, the Duke of Holstein-Gottorp, isn't happy with his independent ways; he is one of the many noblemen in Germany who have turned from the church toward Lutheranism, he can't do anything about our Baron's support for us Mennists. Baron von Ahlefeld has resisted every attempt by him to turn us away.

"In 1553, the same year we came here, I found out through some brothers in the faith where Menno was hiding with his family, and I convinced the Baron that we should invite him to live here in Bad Oldesloe. He agreed to keep him here, so we contacted him through these brothers, and Menno and his family moved to Wuestenfelde, where we also lived. We now have our own bishop and spiritual leader living right here in our neighbourhood. We have even taken the name Mennist in his honour. We plan to build a church soon, and that will complete our dreams."

With that, Father signalled that it was time for the younger ones to go to bed, so the quiet was broken by the bustle of little bodies getting ready for bed, older ones helping young ones to get into their night clothes. Tooth brushing had not yet been invented, but faces and hands were washed, so that pillows and bedding would not be soiled.

# Chapter Three

H enry Derksen made his way quietly from his parents' house-barn combination behind two neighbours' dwellings and walked in his new boots to Bad Oldesloe, to the Hildebrands' house-barn farmstead. It was now 11:30 p.m. on Christmas Eve, and the Derksens had retired to bed. He tapped on the door and waited. The window was frosted, so that it was not possible to see in, though a small candle burned inside. He heard a rustle and withdrew to the area between the barn and the house, where the common entrance was located. In a few moments, a young woman emerged, also dressed for the outdoors. Very soon the elder Hildebrands followed out of the door, and the foursome began their walk into the snowy landscape. Snowflakes drifted soundlessly onto their heavy coats, mittens, scarves and hats.

The Catholic church bells began to ring, and the four made their way along with a number of others to the midnight mass with which the Hildebrand family celebrated this hallowed evening. Henry hoped no Anabaptists would notice him among the parishioners, because it was well known that the Derksens were Mennists and held no social or religious contact with Catholics. But Henry loved Heidi Hildebrand. She was the apple of his eye, the darling of his heart. It would not make much difference to the Catholics, if he attended their service. It was the Anabaptists he was worried about: if they found out he attended a Catholic service, they would be exceedingly upset. That was especially true of his parents, Jacob and Eva Derksen. He might even be subjected to the ban by Menno, which would sever all connections with Heidi and even his own family, until he repented openly before the congregation.

Jacob and Eva were aware of Henry's interest in Heidi, and she was a lovely and charming young woman, whom they would dearly have as a daughter-in-law, except that she was a staunch Catholic. She attended every mass she could, and she was always faithful at confession, doing whatever penance was required by the priest for her sins. She had recently spent all her small savings on an indulgence to release her grandmother out of 100,000 years of purgatory and to seal her own salvation. This was supposed to be money she would use for their wedding. Now it was gone to the church.

The Hildebrands were dear folk, and the Derksens appreciated them very much. Jacob worked for John Hildebrand in the hog barns of the Baron. He was a good worker and knowledgeable about pigs. No one knew better than John what to do when a sow was about to give birth to her litter, and how to assist if there was a problem in the birthing. The Hildebrands also had their own plot of land that the Baron had given them for their own needs, so their situation was very similar to the Derksens. Their daughter would make a fine wife for some young man; the problem was that the young man who seemed the most likely was Henry, and in addition to her being Catholic, she was also going to be penniless.

Henry went through the motions of the service without feeling. He sang AMEN when it was called for, and responded mechanically to the other parts of the liturgy, without any sense of spiritual participation. Heidi, on the other hand, was spiritually drawn to the grandeur of the occasion, with candles, incense and festive robes. The gothic architecture gave a sense of the high and holy, but the upkeep of the church had been neglected, so the effect was largely lost in general shabbiness. The

Baron and his family sat in a special section of the church decorated and furnished by him, in marked contrast to the rest of the church. The priest gave a short and quite rousing homily on what this evening meant, but emphasized the Virgin Mary as the main character. At the critical point in the mass, the priest moved in front of the image to the Virgin that adorned the right chapel, in front of the Baron's section of the church, knelt before it, and recited the Ave Maria prayer. At this, Henry's blood began to boil. Not only had the priest emphasized Mary above Jesus in the homily, he had actually prayed to her image. This was one of the strong points Anabaptists made against the Catholic Church: it practiced idolatry.

The pipe organ resounded with a mournful piece played badly by an untrained older man from the Baron's servants, who was the only one who knew anything at all about the old organ. Several of the young boys could be heard giggling behind the organ façade, as they stepped on the bellows to create the air needed for playing the pipes. When mass was over, Henry and Heidi moved out the side door of the church into the crisp air outside. Few people came out of that door, so they had the cemetery surrounding the church building to themselves.

Huddled in the snow behind a large gravestone, the two lovers clasped each others' mittened hands and spoke in hushed whispers. "Wasn't that a lovely service?" Heidi asked.

"I guess I'm really not sure," ventured Henry slowly, "somehow I feel that Christmas is about the Christ Child, not so much about Mary."

"Without her, there wouldn't have been a Christ Child," Heidi countered.

"She's the channel that brought us the earthly Christ Child, but not the Mother of God, as the priest tried to tell us." Henry was getting agitated. His personal beliefs were being tested, and he knew it, but he did not want to give up Heidi. His heart felt shredded, like the turnips his mother put into the soup sometimes. "In other words, it is Christ who is supposed to be worshiped by Christians, not Mary."

"Didn't the angel Gabriel say to her, 'Hail, thou that art highly favored, the Lord is with thee: blessed art thou among women? That's the Latin for Ave Maria."

"Yes, she was selected for the most important job in the world, to bear the Savior, but that didn't make her the Mother of God." Henry was getting more and more animated.

"If Jesus was God, then Mary is the Mother of God," countered Heidi again. "And she remained a virgin all her life and was taken up to heaven, the priest tells us."

"The Bible, I think, tells us that she had a number of children after she bore Jesus." Henry was beginning to get to the end of his theology here and knew it. It was getting colder, and sitting against a stone didn't help.

"I think we need to get you back to your house before we both freeze to death here. It does seem a bit appropriate, though, to become chilled in a graveyard."

"I guess you're right, Henry, but I'm so glad you came to midnight mass with me tonight. I was afraid your religion wouldn't allow that."

"It doesn't. I came, because I wanted to be with you. I'm beginning to wonder, though, whether you really love me, or Mary more. I really thought I loved you, but your idolatry definitely doesn't fit with my idea of what a Christian should believe. And that probably means that our marriage wouldn't work."

Heidi didn't respond; she was deep in thought. The two picked their way between buildings and around trees, avoiding open spaces as much as possible, until they got to the doorway into the area between the house part and the barn part of the Hildebrand farmstead. The parents had just gotten back from midnight mass themselves and were in their bedroom at the other end of the house, getting ready for bed, so they didn't notice Heidi going into her room.

Henry made as if to go home, but veered back towards the church building they had just left. No one was around, but the smell of incense and quenched candles still hung heavily in the air. The church was never locked in such a small village, so he entered the side door without a problem. Looking around for something heavy and metal, he found a piece of loose railing that suited his purpose well. Moving to the offending idol, he swung the metal rod at the head. The nose broke loose, but other parts were solid stone and larger, so they could not be dislodged. He swung again and took off one ear. With another swing a hand was on the floor, and with that, his passion was exhausted.

He retraced his steps behind the neighbors' barns and around the bushes that separated the Derksen farmstead from the Hildebrands', and stepped quietly into the area between the barn and house in theirs. Soundlessly he climbed the steps to the attic and found the bed that he shared with Jacob and crawled under the down quilt. Although he had anticipated the opportunity to spend some time with Heidi, his heart fell as he thought about the spiritual gulf that separated them. He had told her the truth outright, without holding back his true feelings about her. His reaction to the idolatry surprised him somewhat – he had never thought of iconoclasm before. It had happened so naturally he wondered what else he might be capable of doing, if the right moment presented itself. At the same time, he knew he had done the right thing; *idolatry must be stamped out.* With these thoughts, he drifted off to sleep.

# Chapter Four

Leah Derksen tripped along the central roadway from their village of Wuestenfelde towards Bad Oldesloe, where Janzen's store was located. Everything could be bought there, or ordered for you, if it was not in stock. The service in the store was exceptional; the staff of two were at every beck and call of the village folk, who were a mixture of Catholics, Lutherans and Mennists. The Janzens were Mennists, too, but they had an employee from Bad Oldesloe, Hans Schmidt, son of the local Lutheran pastor. For Leah, this was what made the service at Janzen's Store so special, because Hans was her very special friend. Hans, likewise considered Leah to be his very special girlfriend. He was happy every time Leah came into the store to buy anything, or even when she came in only on the pretext of wanting to buy something.

It was three days after Christmas and everything in the villages was back to its wintertime routines. Father was back working in the Baron's hog barns, Henry was working with Abe Voth in the Baron's carpentry shop, and Jake, as Jacob Jr was generally called, in addition to his job of tending the family's livestock, was laboriously reading the new Bible he had received for Christmas, as well as looking for a steady job. Isaac was busy pushing the wheelbarrow around the rooms of the house, loading and unloading toys and whatever he could find that fit the barrow, and the younger children were clamoring around Mother's legs, as they chased each other and vied for each other's toys.

Mother was trying to do the weekly washing, which was a monumental task at the best of times, but especially difficult in this wintery weather, and with all the children around her in the house. Some things were needed from Janzen's Store, so Leah had been sent to purchase them. Mother knew that this would be an errand lovingly fulfilled, but her heart was heavy. *Why couldn't Leah find a suitable Mennist man for her interests, instead of a Lutheran? Yes, the Lutherans taught salvation by faith in Jesus Christ alone, but they baptized babies that didn't know anything about salvation, stating that this brought them into the family of God. Baptism is supposed to be a sign of an already accomplished salvation, not the way to a future salvation. Am I losing my family one by one back to the heathen?*

"Hello Leah," called Hans cheerily from the ladder on which he was standing to stock shelves, "what brings you here today?"

"We are out of candles, flour and salt," replied Leah, her dark eyes flashing at Hans. Why did her cheeks always insist on flushing each time she saw him, she wondered?

"We're out of wheat flour today, every woman in town must have been doing fine baking for the holiday. Could you take rye flour instead?"

"OK, but it bakes much heavier bread, and we like the lighter white wheat flour better," said Leah with a pout. Having just baked her first successful batch of white Bulki, she was now a bit of an expert in bakery science.

"But rye bread keeps you satisfied much longer," countered Hans playfully. "Rye bread is like when you and I are together, it's much more satisfying than when we're separated"

Their banter continued for some time along this line, until Leah asked abruptly, "What did your father preach about on Christmas Eve?"

"He used the shepherds of Bethlehem to illustrate Jesus as the Good Shepherd," Hans recollected, "but, did you hear what happened in the Catholic Church on Christmas Eve? Someone smashed the image of the Virgin Mary, left pieces of nose, ears and hands all over the floor."

"How could anyone do such a thing?" Leah was astonished and showed it.

"The priest has gotten the magistrates investigating who might have been around after Midnight Mass to do this. The bishop has gotten the Baron all worked up, because he should have provided protection for the Church's property. I certainly hope it isn't someone from around here."

"That's for sure," Leah ventured, "I wonder what they would do to someone who did a thing like that."

"Considering all the problems the Catholic Church has had recently, what with us Protestants splitting off, and then you Anabaptists going even further and condemning infant baptism, some people are getting very aggressive against what they consider the abuses of the church to be. One of those things is idolatry, because the Catholics appear to worship their images of biblical characters and saints as a way for their prayers to be heard by God. They think that these saints have God's ear, when it comes to having their prayers answered." Hans knew both the historical and the theological aspects of the Reformation well, and he loved to analyze situations.

As Hans spoke, Leah suddenly became very still and white. Hans didn't notice, as he was still stocking shelves, but she had become quite nervous. "I think I better get my things, so that Mother can finish making supper."

Hans got the things together, putting them into a bag that Leah had brought with her, counted out the change, and saw her off with a pat on the arm.

Leah hurried out of the store with her shopping bag and followed the road from Bad Oldesloe back to Wuestenfelde. Her mind raced and her face flushed at her brisk walking pace. *Can it be possible? Am*

*I just making connections in my mind, or is it real? How can I find out? Who should I ask? In whom can I confide?* It all seemed too strange, too distant, too bizarre to be so close.

Just up the road a bit farther she spied a figure walking. It was Henry, coming home from his workshop. She hurried even faster, until she could call and let him know she wanted to walk with him. Puffing up to where he waited, she handed the bag of groceries to him, and pulling off her mitten, she took a handkerchief out of her pocket to blow her nose. As she looked at Henry, she could see nothing that would help her with her inner turmoil of thoughts, nor could she see any answer to her questions, especially the question that troubled her. *Should I ask him outright, should I hint at knowing, should I approach the subject obliquely, referring to someone else, someone unknown to both of us?*

"I heard something at the store that bothers me very much," she faltered. "Hans told me that the bishop and the magistrates are looking for someone that knocked the nose, ears and hand off the Virgin Mary in the Catholic Church. Do you know anything about it?"

Henry didn't say anything at all, nor was there any change in his expression. Leah wondered at his silence, but couldn't bring herself to probe further. *Is he hiding something? Is he aware of who did it and is covering it up? Is he not aware of how dangerous such an action is? What will my few friends think? How does God feel about such things? How will Mother and Father react, if Henry was involved? What will Hans think?*

"God does not tolerate idolatry, Leah," began Henry slowly. "Israel had to clean it out of their country time after time. It was time that someone did it here. In the Peasants Revolt, led by Thomas Muentzer, they did it in many churches, and there are reformers who believe it must be done in all churches," he concluded.

"But what will happen now, when the magistrates find the person responsible?" quivered Leah. She still could not bear to ask whether Henry was directly involved. Her thoughts raged on with possible and horrible consequences she had heard about, when others had defied the state system of religion. And that had only been for believing differently, this involved direct action against the Church's property.

"If we truly believe in Christ alone for salvation, we don't need Mary's intervention," continued Henry, "we don't need her image nor her prayers. We have to get rid of this idolatry, or we will fall as Israel did."

"That's true," ventured Leah, getting somewhat braver now, "but in the political climate in which we live, we have always just sort of fitted into whatever was done and simply didn't get involved in the problems of others. We have always run away from them."

"I guess I just got overworked after the Christmas Eve Mass," Henry spoke very softly now, "I was very upset when the priest knelt in front of the statue and prayed to Mary. This was simple idolatry, and I couldn't stand it."

*So my fears were true. Henry was responsible for this. The whole area is looking for him now. What should we do? What should I do? What should I suggest to Henry?* Again her thoughts raced to keep up with her heartbeat. She looked at Henry helplessly, questioningly.

"I will go into hiding," replied Henry, again speaking very softly and reassuringly to his lovely sister. "I'll tell Mother and Father tonight, pack some things and take off."

"But they'll catch you and execute you," she blurted.

"Maybe, but it was for the Lord, and He will protect me, if He wants, and if He wants another martyr, I guess I'll have to be that." Henry's resolve was baffling to Leah. How could he be so calm and assured?

"I have thought a lot about it, even while working in the shop, and I am at peace with God about it." Henry's voice sounded final as though this was his final assertion.

By now they had reached the little village of Wuestenfelde, and soon they were at the door that separated their house from their barn.

"Let me explain to Mother and Father," Henry whispered. Leah nodded and gulped.

Preparations for supper were well underway, but Mother was thankful for the flour, even though it was rye instead of wheat, and hurriedly began stirring it into her batter. Soon a pan of Schnetki was making its way into the oven. They would be a bit heavier than the wheat flour biscuits her family preferred, but they would go well with the meat gravy she had prepared.

Supper went well. No one seemed to notice that Henry and Leah didn't say anything, except the necessary requests for food to be passed and the corresponding thanks that followed. The Schnetki and gravy were a favorite meal of the little ones, and the older ones had also grown to cherish these dishes that had become staples in their diet. The dishes were cleared away, the little ones were prepared for bed, and the older ones began to settle into their evening activities.

"I have something I want to tell all of you," began Henry confidently. "I believe that idolatry must be stamped out, or we will go down as the Israelites did so many times. I am the one who smashed the image of Mary after the Christmas Eve Mass." Henry was animated now, and continued in spite of the shock on his family's faces. "I went with Heidi Hildebrand to the mass after we were finished our family time on Christmas Eve. The priest rambled on about Mary, finally kneeling in front of the statue and praying to her. Heidi and I talked in the cemetery after the mass, and I told her I couldn't stand it that they prayed to Mary instead of Jesus. I even told her that I wondered whether we should get married. After I took her home, the church was empty, so I went back in and smashed the image."

Jacob and Eva looked at each other with fear in their eyes. Jake looked at the floor. No one spoke.

"We have always run away from problems before," began Father, "but now you have taken matters into your own hands and have acted on your beliefs in a very dangerous way. The church does not take kindly to having its property spoiled or taken away. Riches are as important to it as doctrine. Martin Luther also protested against this, and Menno thinks the same. But the bishop and the magistrates must be looking for you right now," he ended, looking around furtively.

"You must hide," interjected Mother.

"The Baron can't protect you against the bishop and the magistrates," added Father.

"Quickly, let's find some things you will need, and you must leave immediately for another prince's domain, perhaps back to Friesland. I hear things have quieted down there." Mother was now racing on, as she began searching for things Henry could pack and take along with him.

Father, too, began to think and search, finding helpful things in nearly every corner and closet.

"I can't carry that much in this weather," protested Henry. "I'll just take a bit to eat and trust that God will lead me to safety. I will try to get work in someone else's shop and not be noticed, if possible," he continued.

Mother's heart was torn for him, and Father's face was grave, as he embraced his eldest son. After embracing each of them in turn, and nodding in the direction of the younger children's beds, Henry slipped out the door into the night.

# Chapter Five

Leah's heart pounded. She found it difficult to go about the household chores. Whether she was tending the younger siblings, helping with the cooking and baking, or doing the mountains of wash that seemingly accumulated overnight, she had her mind on something else. *What was Henry thinking? What was going through his mind, that he would do a thing like that? What is Heidi thinking now? Does she still feel that she had some love left for Henry, after what he did to her beloved Mary? What about Hans? Will he no longer love me?*

"I need to go out to think a bit," she said hesitantly to Mother, knowing that Mother knew all too well what was going through her mind.

"Go ahead, you have worked very hard, and I think everything is done as far as it can be done before supper," Mother answered.

She put on her overcoat and scarf, as well as winter shoes and mitts, finishing with her pretty knitted hat, and left by the door that separated the house from the barn. Plodding up the road toward Bad Oldesloe, she let her thoughts wander.

*What a fine tracery on the overhanging poplar branches. What is Hans thinking about me and our family now? What am I thinking? Do I still love*

*Henry, my dear, dear brother? That was a stupid thing to do. Everyone will be looking for him now, and he will be executed. What a waste of a young and promising life. Watch those ruts in the snow, or you'll be landing in a clumsy heap. What do I really believe? What would I be willing to die for?*

The road was only three kilometers long, but it seemed like hours before she reached Janzen's Store. As she entered, she noticed that Hans was alone at the counter. He looked at her the moment the little bell that tinkled whenever the door was opened rang out, and greeted her with a smile, "Hi Leah. What brings you here again, right after you were here. Did you forget something?"

"I need to talk with you, Hans. Henry told me what he had done, and then he told Mother and Father. Now he has gone into hiding. We'll probably never see him again. If you hadn't told me about what happened in the Catholic church, I would never have suspected anything. Now I'm all confused. It all seems so stupid and unnecessary, but it's done, and there is nothing for it now, except to hide. What will the authorities do to him? What will they do to our family? What will this do to our relationship?" The words seemed to pour out of her. Hans listened quietly, then he came around the counter and put his arms around her.

"Henry did what he did, because he believed in something bigger than himself. He felt that this representation or symbol in the church was holding the people back from a belief in the true Jesus Christ of the season, because their attention was focused from the Savior to Mary, whom they call the Mother of God."

"So you don't hate me because of what he did?"

"Well, maybe I think you put him up to it, so I'm suspicious," he winked.

"Don't do that, Hans. I can't take much more right now," she whimpered. He continued to hold her and found a clean handkerchief to brush the tears from her eyes.

"No, I think Henry acted on his own, without anyone telling him what to do or guiding his thoughts. I know Menno would never get anyone to act like that, and I don't know anyone else that would have put this into his mind. I still love you very much, Leah." His quiet analysis comforted her, and she began to see things in a bit better perspective.

"If the priest gets too upset by this, and the bishop begins interfering with the Baron, there is no telling what will happen. The Baron is responsible for everyone in his estate, Catholics, Lutherans and Mennists alike, and he has to protect each from the other. So far he has been quite successful, but this will definitely upset that balance," Hans continued. "I'm afraid the magistrates will be called upon to find whoever did the damage, and he will have to pay with his life. I suspect that you Mennists will have to restore the image to the church, which will cost a pretty pfennig."

How could Hans see things so clearly? He seemed to know everyone and everyone's way of thinking and how they would react. Leah tried to see things in the broader sense, but her mind was so clogged with thoughts of Henry and the predicament he had gotten himself and their family into, that she couldn't get beyond her own feelings. The only thing that mattered to her in all of this was fact that he still loved her. She clung to him as her last resort.

"I better get back home," she finally said, just as another customer was approaching the door. She quickly wiped the tears from her eyes, gave Hans a squeeze, and made for the door, which was now opened by the new customer. She brushed past the woman without acknowledging her and began tromping back to Wuestenfelde.

• • •

Jake was thunderstruck. *What has my brother done? How could he have taken matters into his own hands and gotten our family into such a predicament? How could he have been so selfish? Didn't he realize that his actions would not just affect his own life, but the lives of everyone in Wuestenfelde? It is pretty obvious how the priest will react. He'll go to the Baron and demand restitution and justice. He'll also report to the bishop, who will probably go*

*to the Baron himself and make the demands. He will also demand that the*
*Mennists be driven from the estate.*

As he wandered toward Bad Oldesloe, his thoughts went in smaller and smaller circles, repeating themselves oftener and oftener. By the time he had reached town, he realized where he was, and saw the great tree in the center of town, its silhouette bare and stark. He headed for it, knowing that a bench had been built around it long ago, and this was a favorite place for people to just sit and think, or to engage in a rendezvous with a lover. He didn't see anyone until he sat down, when he noticed someone on the other side of the great tree, sitting on the same bench, which girded the great stump.

"I'm sorry, I didn't know anyone was here," he blurted. "Who is it?"

"I'm Heidi, and it's OK for you to be here. I would actually like to talk with you, Jacob, if that would be alright with you," said a weary voice.

Jacob got up and walked around the tree to where Heidi was sitting, and sat down beside her. It was strange to sit beside his brother's girlfriend, but somehow it seemed appropriate right now, since both of them shared in a similar situation.

"What was Henry thinking?" she blurted. "He seemed to know that he was going to do this when he left me in the cemetery, but I had no idea. I thought he had enjoyed the Christmas Eve Mass, but he told me then that the fact that the priest prayed to the image of Mary disturbed him very much. It never occurred to me that he would do something so radical after he left me."

"He told all of us when he got home from work today, and he has now gone into hiding," Jake offered.

"He told me that, if I held on to my Catholic beliefs, our relationship was over. I guess it is over, whether I believe that way or not."

"It seems to me that it would have been difficult to get into a real marriage relationship with two opposing belief systems between you," he volunteered.

"I thought we could work things out and that he would join the Catholic Church again. He told me that he had been baptized into the church when he was a baby, so it would not have been too difficult for him to change back," she stated, matter-of-factly, biting her lips after she had said it, "but I guess you're right, it wouldn't have worked. Now what am I supposed to do? The priest will think that I am responsible along with him, so I'll have to clear my own name in the church."

"I think his confession is enough to satisfy everyone that you were not involved, and that he acted on his own. The bigger issue here is what the bishop will want from the Mennists, to pay for the image to be re-instated," he responded dejectedly.

"Oh, I hadn't thought of that," her eyes suddenly grew wide, as she looked Jacob square in the eyes, tears freezing gently on her cheeks. Both of them were silent for a time, thinking of the terrible consequences of Henry's outrageous act.

"I guess I need to get home," mumbled Heidi, "thanks for coming. I needed that."

"I should be getting home, too," said Jake gently. "I'll see you sometime again."

With that the two parted, each going their own way toward their homes.

# Chapter Six

It was Monday morning. Jacob Derksen plodded to Bad Oldesloe to begin his work in the Baron's hog barns. It was a week since Henry had left home and they hadn't heard a thing from him or about him. Anxious thoughts tormented Jacob. *Where is my son? Why did he do such a rash thing? Even if we don't believe in the Catholics' idols, we know we will just suffer bad consequences, if we do anything to them. Just look at Zwickau and Mühlhausen, what they did to those who defaced churches there. Oh, Henry, please look after yourself and don't get caught! Oh, God, please protect him.*

John Hildebrand greeted Jacob somewhat hesitantly and shoved a paper at him when he arrived at the barn. "Our priest gave me this yesterday," he almost questioned. He was of divided opinion about the article he wanted to share with Jacob, not knowing whether the details were all relevant here, or not.

Jacob looked at the paper, but said haltingly, "I don't read German, only some Dutch."

"Here's what it says," said John, "I'll read it for you, then." John Hildebrand said. He began to read about the magistrates catching a Henry Derksen just as he left the area controlled by Duke Adolf von

Holstein-Gottorp to go into Hamburg, which was an independent city in the Hanseatic League. They were holding him in a jail in Hamburg, waiting for the bishop of Holstein to bring charges against him.

"Henry attended the Christmas Eve Mass together with us, and Heidi and Henry talked about the image after the service," continued John without stopping when he had finished the article. "She said that Henry told her that they could not marry, because Heidi refused to stop praying to Mary. Henry must have gone back afterwards and smashed our beloved Mary." John was showing obvious emotion, as he considered the gravity of the situation. Jacob sat in stunned silence on the feeding cart, not being able to get his mind around the fact that his eldest son was in jail for a crime against the Church.

"I must go home and talk with Eva," Jacob blurted. "The Baron will have to understand that I must deal with family matters."

"The Baron has been very generous to you Mennists, but he can't protect you, when you do things like that," John reprimanded.

Jacob trudged out of the barn and somehow found his way down the road to Wuestenfelde and his house-barn. Eva was shocked to see him come in the door, and saw immediately that something was very wrong. Jacob's eyes were sunken, his face was drawn, and his lip quivered.

"They caught Henry," he blurted.

Eva sat down, wide-eyed and getting whiter. She pulled her apron over her face and began to sob uncontrollably. "They'll kill him," she shrieked.

"Now Eva," Jacob began bravely enough, but his own heart gave out just then, and he also began to weep loudly. Unconsciously, they reached for each other, and soon they stood in the middle of the room in a tight, sobbing embrace, seeking solace in each others' arms.

"We must trust in our Lord," Jacob searched for ways to comfort himself, so that he could comfort his dear wife, who had already witnessed so many of the things that had happened to those who went against the system, even though their conscience told them that the system was wrong.

Just then, Leah and Jake came in. They stood silently at the door, wondering what had brought Father home so early, and why he and Mother were standing there weeping.

"Has something happened to Henry?" asked Leah, premonitorily.

"He's in prison in Hamburg," replied her father, sniffing, looking hard at the floor. "The bishop will go down and state his case against him, and then there will be a trial."

Stunned, Leah and Jake stood there. Henry in prison. Why, he was such a loving and kind person, a *Mustermann* of Christian virtue. All his brotherly acts came flooding into their memory. *What about Heidi, did she know,* Leah wondered? *What about Hans, did he know,* Jake wondered?

"Was there anything about when the trial will start?" asked Jake. "We should try to be there, or at least visit Henry in jail," he continued tentatively.

"Then we would all fall into their hands, and we'd all suffer the same fate," replied Jacob dejectedly.

"I think I could get to Hamburg without being found out," volunteered Jake. "I think it would be good if at least one person from the family was there for him."

"How would you do that?" queried Mother.

"It would be best to ride in a wagon with a load bound for the city, and hide under the stuff," thought Jake.

By now they were all into the conversation, trying to figure out a way for Jake to be at the trial without being discovered. Perhaps he should disguise himself to make himself less conspicuous, one thought. Perhaps he could go to visit a relative in the city, another thought, and simply appear in the crowd that there was sure to be at the trial.

"I like that idea," said Jake. "I could visit Uncle Aron and Aunt Katharina in Altona. I might be able to get to the trial, or at least be near enough to hear what went on there, and maybe get a glimpse of Henry. Maybe he will even recognize me, and that would give him courage."

The plan seemed good to everyone, so Jake began to make plans to go to Hamburg. The rest would try to follow the proceedings from the gossip at Janzen's Store. Perhaps Heidi could help them with that. Surely she still had some feelings for Henry.

Jake found that a load of wool was going from Fresenburg estate to Hamburg the next day, and he believed he could somehow get under the bales and remain undetected. Mother prepared some food for him to take along, and made sure he had the address of his relatives. There was no way of informing them he was coming, but people always expected company, so they would be ready.

The thought that her second son could also be caught suddenly occurred to Mother, and she sat down hard in the nearby kitchen chair, wringing her hands. "God will protect me," whispered Jake. "I don't look at all like Henry. He looks more like Father, and I look more like you, so that will help them not to notice me."

With preparations for Jacob's departure complete, the house began to settle in for the evening meal of baked ham and rye bread, with some cabbage that had been in their root cellar since harvest. There was little conversation, so as not to alert the younger ones to the impending departure. Father prayed out loud that God would bless Henry and each one in the family in turn, and that He would nourish them all with this food, to which all said a hearty Amen.

With supper eaten, the evening wore on with routine tasks and activities, and then everyone went to bed. Jake was not the only one who had difficulty getting to sleep, but he finally drifted off, as did the others.

Early in the morning the rooster's crowing awakened Jake, and he got dressed for traveling in winter. He ate some bread and butter that Mother had gotten ready for him the night before, along with some fried Jreiven, picked up his bundle and slipped quietly out the door. Making his way to Bad Oldesloe, he found where the men were loading the wagon with bales of wool. When no one seemed to be looking, he slipped between the bales and made himself as comfortable as possible.

The wagon was finally loaded, the paperwork completed, and the driver and his assistant mounted their seat. Taking the reins, the driver clicked his tongue to get the horses moving, and they were on their way.

The more than forty kilometers could not be completed in one day, so they stopped at an inn along the way. Jacob remained under the bales until it was dark and went out to see about meeting his human needs. When he had also eaten something, he crawled back between the bales and went to sleep. He was awakened when the wagon began moving the next morning, and remained in his place all day, as they progressed towards Hamburg.

When they entered the city, he heard the men talking about what they were seeing and where they still had to go to reach their destination, which happened to be right next to Altona, the village just to the west of the city, where Jacob's relatives lived. Jacob kept his ears tuned to the men's conversation to determine where they were, and when he deemed it right, he slipped out from between the bales unnoticed and dropped off the back of the wagon. As he began to walk, he took on a nonchalant air, pretending to be just another pedestrian, and no one took particular notice of him walking towards Altona. As he came into the village, he asked another pedestrian where to find Kleine Roosen Strasse, where his uncle and aunt lived. With that, he found their house quite quickly and was welcomed in.

"What brings you here," was their first question.

"I needed to take care of some family business at the courthouse in Hamburg," Jacob tried to evade the real issue, but at the same time, to open the door to ask for help in getting where he wanted to go.

"Uncle Aron is going into Hamburg tomorrow, so you can go along with him," said Aunt Katharina. "You must be hungry after such a long trip. Did you do it in one day?"

"No, we took two days. I rode along with some people from Bad Oldesloe who were bringing wool into the city."

That seemed to satisfy his relatives, so he didn't volunteer more. Supper preparations were already underway, and Aunt Katie, as she preferred to be known, added sufficiently to her ingredients to account for Jacob's ravenous appetite.

"How are things going for the Mennists in Bad Oldesloe? We have heard that Baron von Ahlefeld is very helpful to you there. That's certainly better than we find it here, where it seems that everyone in Hamburg is against us. Luckily, we find it easier here in Altona, where there isn't so much distrust and hatred. It is part of Holstein-Gottorp, so has a Protestant Duke in charge. Still, we must keep a very low profile, or the authorities would drive us out, as well." Uncle Aron was becoming far too inquisitive for Henry's liking.

"Yes, Baron von Ahlefeld has been very good to us. That hasn't made it easy, just possible, to get a new start. Over the past three years we have gained both his confidence and our own sense of self-worth and self-confidence. Menno is now living among us, and is also protected by the Baron," Jake ventured. "We men are able to work in his shops and care for his livestock, and each family has a plot of land on which to raise whatever crop we want for ourselves. We also got a cow, a pig and some chickens from him, so we can build our own farm and have our basic needs supplied. Our sow had a big litter, so we have been blessed with lots of meat, and our garden produced plenty of vegetables to carry us through the winter. Our cow gives lots of milk, and her calves have grown quite big. The heifers will be big enough to breed in another year, so our increase will become faster. We have a building in which to hold church services, and we are considering building a proper church. The community is still mixed, so we get some opposition, and some of us tend to set them off in one way or another with our expressions of worship. But that's also the case between Lutherans and Catholics."

The evening wore on, as Aunt Katie wanted to know about each of the family members in turn, and Jake sought ways to evade giving away his purpose for coming to the city, saying that Henry had left home to look for work elsewhere, which was true. Finally, Jake was shown to the couch on which he would have to sleep, as the house was very small and had only two rooms. Everyone turned in for the night, and the lamps were blown out.

Breakfast over, Uncle Aron and Jake harnessed the horse to the small wagon and headed eastward along the Elbe River into the city of Hamburg. Jacob had never seen such huge buildings. The wharf was also extremely interesting. Jacob got off near the center of town and thanked his uncle for the hospitality and the ride, and stated that he would find his own way back to Bad Oldesloe from there. Nothing seemed to have disturbed his uncle's thoughts about the purpose of Jacob's visit to Hamburg, and Jacob had not had to lie. He had just avoided telling the whole truth.

Jacob asked someone where the courthouse was and had it pointed out among the great buildings in the center of town. The cases to be tried were listed on a board near the entrance, along with the room number and the time of the trial, so he made a mental note to go to room 305 at 11:00 a.m. This gave him a good hour to explore the downtown area, which had many places of interest. The fashions in the windows disturbed his simple tastes, for they, especially those for young women, revealed more, it seemed, than they covered. He could not imagine Leah wearing anything so daring, nor would he want her to do that.

As 11:00 o'clock approached, Jacob joined a small group of onlookers crowding into the small courtroom. The judge entered, and the bishop and his legal advisor appeared at their table. Henry was led out of a back room with his hands tied behind him and forced into a chair beside the judge's desk. With that, the proceedings began. Henry looked down at the floor, so he did not notice Jacob in the group.

The bishop's legal advisor explained to the judge the nature of the charge. The judge asked the bishop whether the charge was what had been stated, to which the bishop agreed. Then the judge asked Henry whether he had anything to say in his defense. Henry continued to look down at the floor.

"You must answer my questions, young man," the judge snapped, "now, did you, or did you not do this damage to the church property in Bad Oldesloe?" he asked quite forcefully.

Henry seemed dazed, so he hesitated. "May I say something about this thing?" he stalled.

"You have been asked to say something, now say it," the judge snapped again.

"I was raised mostly in Holland, so I speak High German poorly," Henry began, and he slowly looked up and saw Jake in the crowd. Fortunately for both, he didn't let on that he knew anyone in the courtroom. Jake's presence, however, gave him new courage, and he continued, "We, that is we Mennists, believe that the Bible teaches us not to worship idols. We think that the Catholics' prayers to Mary, especially to her image, are idolatry. When I saw the priest kneel before her statue on Christmas Eve and pray to her, I couldn't help it, I became very angry inside at this idolatry. My girlfriend and I discussed it after the service, and she felt that this was a totally correct way to worship God. I disagreed, and we broke off our friendship."

The judge listened intently, as did the bishop and his lawyer. Everything he had said about the Mennists' attitude towards Catholic idolatry was true, but he had not admitted to damaging the statue of Mary.

The lawyer stood up. "May I question the suspect, please, your honour?" he asked the judge. When assent had been given, he walked over to Henry, and looking at him very hard, he almost shouted, "Did you knock the nose, ears and hands off the statue in the Catholic church in Bad Oldesloe on Christmas Eve?"

Henry looked hard back at him, looked around the courtroom, and began to speak. "I believe that God will look at what the Catholics are doing with such statues and judge them, just as I am being judged for my faith right now."

"Answer the simple question," bellowed the bishop.

"I do not believe that it can be proven that I did the damage you speak about," Henry responded softly. "No one, apparently, saw it being done."

"We are asking you a simple question, did you or did you not do it?" bellowed the lawyer.

"I believe that Jesus will reward those who live out their faith in Him, and will give them the crown of life," responded Henry. "But He will not reward those who have perverted their faith by adding in all kinds of traditions that were taught by people rather than the Bible, and He will not accept people who trust in such traditions instead of trusting Him personally into His heaven. I do not believe that baptizing babies makes them children of God. Baptism must be a sign of something that has happened in a person's life, not a way to reach that goal."

"Quit preaching and answer the question," thundered the judge. "Did you damage the image of Mary in that church on that night?"

Henry bowed his head, "Yes," he whispered intently.

The crowd gave a gasp and became deathly still. Jacob's heart nearly stopped, and he looked intently at Henry, to see whether Henry would look at him in return. He did not, but looked up to the ceiling instead, as if pleading with God for His help. The bishop and the lawyer gloated over their triumph. The judge looked long and hard at Henry, then at the bishop, and back to Henry, before he spoke.

"Because you have admitted to the crime of defacing Church property, I sentence you to be beheaded by the magistrate appointed to that task." Henry's skin whitened, but his face was unmoving. His gaze fastened for an instant on Jacob in the crowd, then on the bishop, the lawyer, and finally directly on the judge, who continued, "You will be taken immediately to the place of execution. I pronounce this case closed."

There was another gasp from the crowd, Henry was led out, and the crowd burst into discussion. Most seemed in favor of the sentence, for they strongly believed in the state's protection of church property, regardless of which faction was involved. Jacob followed in the crowd, as it made its way down the three flights of stairs to the street below, and he continued to follow it, as it wound its way through several back streets to a somewhat secluded square, where the executioner already stood waiting, his huge sword gleaming in the noonday sun.

As Henry was brought before the executioner, he turned and shouted, "May this be an example to you. If you continue to worship idols, or to believe in the words of men, rather than the words of God, you are lost forever. I will get a martyr's reward for sticking to my faith, regardless of the price. Don't lose out on salvation, because some priest who is bound to some pope says it should be otherwise. Believe the Bible, not men. I am ready, and I say farewell to my family and my loved ones, and say hello to my Savior and Lord Jesus Christ."

At this the magistrates pushed Henry toward the executioner, who made him kneel by his chopping block and place his head over it. Henry offered no resistance, except to raise his eyes to heaven in a final prayer, before the executioner finished his grisly task. Again, the crowd gasped. Jake almost fainted, but caught himself and sat down on a low stone wall nearby. As the crowd disbursed, he noticed that the magistrates were looking at him, so he also left the scene.

His thoughts were filled with the awful scene, but his heart rejoiced in Henry's faithful testimony. This would help his family and others in the Mennist colony in Bad Oldesloe to rejoice in Henry's death.

# Chapter Seven

M enno Simon's message was simple and clear: As true believers, we will always face a hostile world that wants to do away with anything that reminds them of the only way to cleanse themselves of their sin. Henry Derksen had chosen to be faithful to his beliefs, and he had paid the ultimate price for doing so. At the same time, he had earned a special reward from his Savior for becoming a martyr for the faith.

The Derksen family sat quietly on the front benches, boys on the left side and women and girls on the right side, facing the deacons, with Jacob as one of them, seated across the right side of the front. There were a couple of hymns sung in unison, without instrumental accompaniment, but led by Vorsaenger, also seated along the left front wall on a bench. Menno, in his long black frock coat and high black boots, stood behind a wooden pulpit, propped up by his cane, to preach. Everyone was dressed simply, in dark colors, some blue, some grey, but mostly black.

The service made a lasting impression on everyone, for it commemorated the first martyrdom in their Bad Oldesloe community, and the last one in a long line of martyrdoms since the Anabaptists had begun to challenge established beliefs of the Catholic Church, and even to challenge the beliefs of fellow Protestants. Especially repugnant to the two major church divisions was the Mennists' belief that infant baptism was of no avail for the child's salvation, but that baptism must be a sign of a true faith in Christ for salvation. Such occasional fits of iconoclasm, as evidenced by Henry, were also dealt with severely. Most martyrdoms had occurred, because of being "re-baptized" into the Mennist religion, thus renouncing the infant baptism practiced by the established churches.

Because there was no body to bury, there was no after-service at the cemetery. Everyone simply went to their homes. The Derksens trudged along with everyone to their own home and quietly went inside. The weather, though it was winter, was quite cheery, so the walk was not hindered by severe cold or heavy snow. No conversation broke the silence. Each one was left alone with individual thoughts. As they entered the house and began to hang up their winter coats, Isaac asked the obvious: "Why did they talk about Henry in the church?" His underdeveloped brain just couldn't grasp what had transpired.

Jake, now the eldest son and brother, took it upon himself to try to explain in simple language to his handicapped young brother what a martyr was.

"Then Henry won't come home anymore," ventured Isaac, as the truth of it all dawned on him.

"We will see him again in heaven," said Mother comfortingly through her tears, "but here on earth we will never see him again."

Even Miriam could understand that, and smiled. Then she, too, clouded up and began to sob.

Emotions ran high all day, as each one dealt with grief and hope alternately. Menno and Gertrude came to visit the family then, offering comfort over a simple Faspa meal of Tweiback, butter and jam, with some Pirps, a hot drink made with roasted grain, dried chicoree and boiling water, to drink. Gertrude brought a bouquet of winter branches neatly tied with a bow. They talked about the times of the New Testament, when early Christians also paid with their lives to spread the faith. Henry was in good company, along with the apostles of Jesus Christ and Paul, who wrote many New Testament books. He had 'fought a good fight, he had finished his course, he had kept the faith: henceforth there would be laid up for him a crown of righteousness, which the Lord, the righteous judge, shall give him at that day.' Menno recounted how the massacre of his brother and 300 others in Bolsward had brought him to the true faith, and hoped that Henry's martyrdom would bring others to true faith in Jesus Christ. The Derksens said AMEN to that, and the Simons left.

• • •

Menno and Gertrude stayed up late after their visit to the Derksens. *What shall be done about reformist people who go beyond that which society allows? Were they wrong in their zeal? What is the biblical answer to all of this? What will the Baron do now about our living on his property?* Menno left the house to go to the Menno Cottage, a house the Baron had made available to him for his printing press. Here he published one tract after another. He would write another one on the benefits of non-resistance, rather than open rebellion against the foes of true Christianity.

All they that take the sword shall perish with the sword: This passage from Matthew's gospel came to mind. Although the sword is different from the hammer, they can both be used as weapons. Whatever is used as a weapon instead of trusting completely in the Lord's power to deliver is all the same, he reasoned. Attacking the enemy's property or attacking his person is no different: both are equally wrong. Therefore, he must teach his followers not to use violence in any form to defend the gospel, but to leave all defense of persons or doctrine to the Lord. Simply proclaiming the truth would save the world, not seeking to bring in the Kingdom of God by force, as they had tried in Muenster twenty-three years before, and Zwickau forty-three years before.

Menno returned to his house and joined his wife in bed, but couldn't sleep. Gertrude, also unable to sleep, prayed earnestly, "God in heaven, please help us all to live our lives for you in quietness and confidence, as you wish, and be with Menno, as he wrestles with these great thoughts. Also, be with the Derksens tonight, and show them the way forward."

• • •

Baron Bartholomew von Ahlefeld also couldn't sleep. He had heard about the martyrdom of Henry and its cause. He had been well aware of the nature of his crime, for the image was close to the area in the church reserved for him and his family, and he could see the damaged statue every time he went to worship. He was also acutely aware that the practice of praying to the image was not in keeping with a belief in the triune God. Mary and the saints were not part of that trinity, so why should we pray to them? He had Catholic, Lutheran and Mennist subjects living on his estate and working for him, and he was above all a man of peace. He wanted no sectarian violence. Although he couldn't make up his mind to leave the Church, he knew that the Protestants and possibly even the Anabaptists were right in their doctrine, so he supported them as best he could by protecting them from the Emperor and the Bishop. This duplicity took its toll on his spirits, and tonight he was tormented by his thoughts.

*Now, this radical has done something that upsets the whole serenity of the situation. What should I do? Should I expel the Mennists as iconoclasts? Should I allow the Lutherans to remain? They, too, were iconoclasts in the Peasant War, forty-three years ago, so can I trust them now? They all seem pretty placid now, except for this one incident, so perhaps I could risk further support for them. Still, I should talk with Menno Simons and inform him that the Mennists' being allowed to remain on my property is contingent on their being law-abiding citizens. No overt acts of rebellion against established order will be tolerated, and no conversions from one religion to another, nothing that will upset the status quo of a peaceful, productive society within my estate. Yes, the status quo is the best plan,* he thought, and drifted contentedly to sleep.

• • •

The priest of the Catholic Church in Bad Oldesloe, Father Daniel, was concerned about the look of his church building, especially the desecrated image of Mary that still stood there as a reminder of what had transpired. Having won the court case and seeing the culprit pay with his life was somewhat satisfying, but he was still left wondering how he was to replace the statue. Just then Bishop Paulus came by to the church manse to discuss what should be done about replacing the statue.

"I think the Mennists should restore the statue," he began, "It was one of them that destroyed it, and the Derksen family and the Mennist group need to replace it."

"These people have no money, and a new statue would cost 50 ducats to cast," said Father Daniel. "Besides, the Baron is protecting them from anything that we plan while they are on his estate."

"I have spoken to the Baron, and he has agreed that the Mennists are to be held responsible," said the bishop. "It will be very difficult for them, and we might have to wait for a while for them to raise the money, but they can be made to do so. The bishopric can forward you the money until then, and you may go ahead and have a new bronze statue cast."

"Will you also speak with Menno, then?" asked the priest, who thought it might be more impressive, if the bishop spoke to him, than if he spoke to him. As he spoke, he fidgeted with his surplice nervously.

"That would give him too much credibility. He's not worth having a visit from the bishop," the self-important church official declared, his nose high in the air and his hand waving menacingly. "You need to speak with him, to demand repayment for property damage to your church building. You can also tell him that the Baron agreed not to allow anyone in his estate to convert from one religion to another. We cannot have our people leaving us to join with these heretics, especially not some ecstatic ones who sympathize with what this Derksen boy has done." His pudgy fingers counted out the points he wanted to make with the local priest, who cowered before him.

Father Daniel was not excited about meeting with Menno, for he feared his popularity in the community, but he reluctantly agreed to do so. He did want his church to look appealing to the parishioners, and he certainly didn't want anyone to leave his congregation; the budget would not allow that.

"I will see him later today," he said, as the bishop put his greatcoat over his bishop's garb and looked out the door to see that his carriage was waiting for him. He left immediately after the bishop had departed, to see if Menno was in his printing cottage.

• • •

Eva fretted her way through the day's routines. Her small ones and Isaac demanded her attention at all hours, so she had no time for thoughts of her own, except as she plodded through the daily chores. Now, as she lay in her bed beside Jacob, who was lost in his own thoughts, she allowed her mind to wander. *How could my own eldest son have done such a rash thing? He had maintained a good testimony through it all, except in getting too excited about taking matters into his own hands, but that doesn't restore him. He will forever be a memory to me, nothing more. He hadn't even had a chance to begin his own family. There will be no one to carry on the family name he would have given. There will be no grandchildren from his line, that I could cuddle and knit for. His relationship with Heidi wasn't what she wanted, either, but you have to let your grown-up children make up their own minds, even about who to marry. Maybe she would have converted, and that would have solved the whole riddle.*

She continued on this line for some time, but finally sleep found its way into her mind and body, and she continued her thoughts in nightmares, twisting and turning through the night, and fighting for covers as the cold of night settled in.

# Chapter Eight

The next few days went by as a winter mist for the Derksen family. Each one wrestled with the increasing and awful reality of Henry's death. Only necessary requests or comments were made. Each one went back to work to face whatever hostility or sympathy should come from their fellow workers.

Jacob went back to the Baron's hog barn to meet John Hildebrand, who had already shown his ambivalence about Henry's action, when he had read the article to him, describing Henry's crime and capture. Jacob expected scorn and ridicule, but he had set his heart to be brave and not to retaliate, if harsh words were spoken.

John saw Jacob coming into the barn and nodded for him to come over to where he was. Jacob thought, *here comes a tongue-lashing.* Instead, John grasped his hands and looked into Jacob's eyes intently.

"I am terribly sorry about Henry," he began, "I can't even imagine what it must be like for you to lose your eldest son."

"He did it because he believed in something bigger than himself," Jacob ventured tentatively.

As the morning wore on and the work progressed, Jacob wondered what had come over John, that he was so sympathetic. As the men stopped in the feed room, which in spite of the grain dust everywhere was the cleanest place in the barn, to unpack their boxed lunches, Jacob instinctively bowed his head to thank the Lord for his food, and John bowed his head with him. They began to eat in silence.

After a few minutes, John began again. "I've thought a lot about Henry and what he did and why. Heidi was quite upset when she found out Henry had destroyed Mary's image, and she thought back on their conversation in the graveyard, she says. She was terribly upset that Henry would rather hold to his beliefs than to hold onto her. We've talked about it as a family, too, and we began to question what the Church was teaching us about faith. We also realized that, when we were baptized as babies, we didn't even know it was happening, so how could we have faith. We began to discuss also what it meant to pray to Mary and to pray to saints and images, and we could see that this only leads us away from true faith in Jesus Christ. We would like to talk to Menno Simon, if we can."

Jacob nearly fell off the feeding pail he was sitting on. Henry's testimony was already bearing fruit! "I will talk with Menno tonight, and see if he can come by to your house tomorrow evening," he said. John seemed pleased that Jacob would go to such trouble for him, and they went back to caring for the hogs in the barn.

After work, Jacob stopped by Menno's Cottage and told him about the Hildebrand family's wanting to talk about faith in Jesus Christ. Menno promised to go and see them the next evening. Jacob said he would tell John at work the next day that Menno was coming that evening.

When he got home, Jacob was beaming. This was a great contrast to the expressions he saw on his wife's face and on those of his children. They had obviously been in mourning all day. As Eva and Leah got supper on the table, Jacob told the family about the Hildebrands' interest in talking with Menno. He got quite animated, as he told them that this had come about because of Henry's sacrifice. That brought some nods of appreciation from the older ones in the family, as they realized what Henry's martyrdom was bringing to their community.

"I'll talk to Heidi," Leah said brightly. "She might appreciate it, if I try to befriend her." The others nodded their approval at this new burst of missionary zeal on her part. "I'll talk to Hans about this, too, and maybe he'll understand."

The evening went by much more easily than the day had, as the family shared in the chores and then played a simple table game together. The younger ones were more contented, now that they saw the relaxed expressions on the older ones' faces. Although the atmosphere was still somewhat subdued, the family was coming to grips with the impact of their situation.

• • •

Leah again went to the store in Bad Oldesloe. As she greeted Hans, she noticed that he was a bit hesitant in his replies to her. "Is something wrong? What's bothering you?" she asked. She thought that he was holding a grudge because of the circumstances of Henry's death, which was a well-known fact in the community by now.

"I've been meaning to tell you, but with all the other things that have been going on, I haven't been able to," he replied softly. "I have decided to go to Wittenberg and study for the ministry, like my father," he continued. "I'm worried that this will keep us apart too much and for too long, but it is what I feel I must do."

Leah looked at him in amazement. *Hans, a student, away from home, and far away from me.* Her heart sank, as she contemplated the loneliness ahead of her for the next number of years. Then the thought of being a pastor's wife crossed her mind. This was quite a bit to absorb in one brief encounter, especially while she was now deeply in mourning.

"I hope you don't mind, but I asked Mr. Janzen if you could take my place working in the store," Hans continued. "That would give you something to do each day, and it would provide you with a bit of income."

Leah had been wondering whether there was anything she could do to earn something, but her thoughts had drifted to being a nanny in a rich person's home, or helping in the hospital laundry, or perhaps working in the bakery – things that related to what she had done at home. Again, all of this was coming a bit quickly, so she couldn't speak.

"You're not angry with me, are you?" questioned Hans.

"No, no, no, this is all just coming a bit too quickly," she responded brokenly. "I think I can see why you would want to study for the ministry, and I am interested in finding some work, but to have you gone for so long, that's something to digest."

"I will still be able to come home during university breaks, so the time will be broken up into shorter segments," he offered.

"When will you be leaving?"

"The winter semester begins in two weeks, so I will be packing and getting ready to go right away. Could you start work next week?"

"I will need to ask my parents, but I don't think they would object to my working in the store, and I think I would enjoy it," she pondered. Life was throwing too many changes into her life all at once, and this was all just too overwhelming for a simple country girl like Leah. "Can we meet after work tonight? I have something I want to talk about with you," she added, almost as an afterthought, though this was what she had actually come for.

"Certainly. Under the bare old linden tree, as usual?" he said.

She nodded, smiled, and left the store to walk home. There was plenty of time during that walk for her to process her thoughts about Hans's vocation and her new calling. She would be able to convince her parents that this was what God wanted for her right now.

• • •

Jake contemplated what his life should be like, now that he was the eldest son. He finished the chores and came in for breakfast, which consisted of bread with pork Jreiven (cracklings) and Prips. He didn't say much, but his mind was racing. Not being outgoing by nature, he did not feel he should go into something like the ministry or teaching. Besides, those would require further schooling, and the family simply couldn't afford to send him away to school. He would need to help bring in some income. Perhaps he could get on where Henry had worked, in the Baron's carpentry shop. He would enjoy that.

"I wonder whether I could get to work in the Baron's carpentry shop where Henry worked," he broached the subject with his mother. "I think Mr. Voth would accept me to work there."

"It would probably be good for you to have a job. Whether working in the same shop where Henry worked is a good idea is another matter. I guess you could give it a try and see what Mr. Voth says."

After breakfast he dressed and left the house to walk to Bad Oldesloe, where he entered the shop and looked around for Mr. Voth. Finding him instructing an apprentice in the art of shaving a spoke for a wheel, he asked if he could speak with him. The man nodded and left the young man to finish his work.

"I would like to take Henry's place in your shop," began Jacob with great hesitation.

"Henry was a good worker. Too bad he had to go overboard in his religion," the foreman stated. "I could use another good man, and I expect you will work as hard as Henry did. You stay out of trouble, though, or I'll have to let you go. Go to Horst over there," he pointed to a man assembling a wagon, "and tell him that you are starting today."

Jake was amazed that he could start at all, let alone start immediately, but he went quickly to where the wagon was, and offered his help. Horst looked at him and nodded, pointing to an axle that needed to be brought to him. So Jake now had a job. He had brought no lunch, but he was sure his spirits would carry him through the day.

• • •

The next weekend the Derksens were happy to have the Hildebrands over for Sunday dinner. Heidi was their youngest and the only child still at home, and John and his wife were somewhat older than Jacob and Eva, but their various common connections seemed to give them many things to talk about. The younger children ate their food separately beforehand and went about playing in the back room, and then the older ones sat around the table to talk.

"We had a good talk with Menno Simons and Gertrude the other night," began Mrs. Hildebrand, who now asked to be addressed as Lizzy. "They were very kind and didn't attack our beliefs at all. They simply said what you people believe, and we were able to understand much better what the differences are. He did say, though, that the Baron had warned him that no one in the estate is allowed to change his religion. "Now we don't know what to do."

Everyone looked crestfallen. *How will it be possible for the Hildebrands to express their true beliefs, if they are not able to be baptized into the Mennist faith?* Heidi wondered about something else.

"We had to live a divided life, too," said Jacob, to break the silence. "We remained members of the Catholic Church long after we had begun to attend secret meetings of the Anabaptists in Witmarsum. When we decided to get baptized by them, we had to flee, as Menno and his family did."

Just then the evening was interrupted by a knock at the door. It was Menno Simon himself. He entered the room, leaning heavily on his cane, to where everyone was seated around the table and looked around at the Derksen family and the Hildebrand family.

"I don't want to disturb your evening, but I need to speak with you alone," said, gesturing to Jacob. Together they went into an adjacent room and talked earnestly for a while. Then they both came back into the main room. Then Menno left the house, and the two families were left once again to look at each other.

"What did Menno want to tell you," asked Eva, clearly curious, as all were.

"I can tell you, it was just that he didn't want to involve the Hildebrands in our family's private affairs, or our affairs as a congregation, since they were not part of either. Now, since that seems to be changing, I can tell you all. The Catholic Church is demanding 50 ducats for the replacement of the statue of Mary that Henry smashed. We are personally responsible for it, according to the Baron, but Menno said that the congregation would take on its share of the cost. Altogether, if each family sells one heifer or three piglets, we can come up with enough to cover the damages. We are also warned by the Baron, that no such behavior will be tolerated on his estate, and that we must not do anything against any other religion, or he will withdraw his protection, and we will have to leave. So, that is what Menno said to me."

This brought a new dimension to the conversation, in which all could join heartily for the rest of the evening. As the Hildebrands got ready to leave, they expressed their great sadness for the Derksens in losing their son, but also gave hope to the cause for which he had died. They prepared to leave for home, and John went to the barn to get the horse and sled ready for their return trip. Lizzy and Heidi said their farewells all around, and they left to climb into the sled for the drive to Bad Oldesloe.

*How will each one of us react to the new stipulations for our faith? Will we choose not to convert to Mennism, having seen what it would cost? Where does each one in the Derksen family stand in regards to their faith, especially as it revolves around the practice of it in public and in relationship to others in the community?* With a mixture of thoughts, the Hildebrands drove their sled home and the Derksens prepared for bed.

# Chapter Nine

Leah woke early the next morning. Something was bothering her. Her mind couldn't get rid of it. It kept going round and round. As she lay in bed, she formed her plan. *It is another few days before I will begin work in Janzen's store, and another week before Hans leaves for Wittenberg to study. I must act quickly. My family must not know, for they would certainly not approve, and I do not want interference from my parents or my brother Jake. Now, how can I accomplish this without raising too much suspicion?*

Following breakfast cleanup, Leah left for Bad Oldesloe. This was regular enough that no one was concerned at all. Hurriedly, she walked the three kilometers in the snow that had fallen overnight. In her hurry, she didn't even stop to make snow angels or to walk patterns into the white layer on the ground. Her steps were straight and her direction clear. Before long she was at the unfamiliar door of Pastor Schmidt, who beckoned her in, knowing her from her relationship with Hans. She had never been in their home before, but she was welcomed heartily and warmly by him and Mrs. Schmidt.

"What brings you here?" queried Pastor Schmidt, smiling broadly at her.

"I want to be baptized into the Lutheran Church," stated Leah, confidently.

"Were you not baptized already?" asked the pastor. "Come, let's go into the parlor to talk about this." He led the way to a smaller room off the main hallway.

"My parents were always on the run as I was born, and they didn't believe in baptizing babies, so I have never been baptized at all," she responded. "After all that has happened lately, I am not interested in throwing my lot in with my parents and the Mennists. They have such strong beliefs, and someone like Henry goes off and does what he did. They think it was a marvelous demonstration of true faith; I think it was foolish and unnecessary. I believe that Jesus died for our sins and there is no other way to heaven, but I don't think the Mennists way is the only way as a church."

"Is there any other reason you want to cast your lot in with us Lutherans," the pastor probed.

"You know that Hans and I are very close friends, and that we'll probably marry some day, when he finishes his studies and takes a church, so I want to be there for him as a good pastor's wife."

This wasn't exactly news to the pastor, who suspected it all along, but he had been wondering how his son's marriage to a Mennist would affect his ability to minister in a Lutheran church. He and his wife were impressed with Leah as a fine woman, who would make a good wife for their son. *If it were not for these accursed divisions among believers,* he mused. *The Eastern Church divided from the Western Church over the Pope. Luther divided the church on the basis of salvation by faith alone, and not additional works. Zwingli divided the Protestant Church on the basis of the Eucharist, and the Mennists and other Anabaptists divided it on the basis of baptism. Is there no end to what can divide God's Kingdom?*

These musings took some time, and meanwhile Leah sat looking earnestly at the pastor for some sign to ease her anxiety.

"Your parents will not be happy with your decision, Leah," ventured the pastor tentatively. "Just like we Lutherans, your people tend to stay together as families."

"Yes, I have thought of that. I am going to take Hans's job in the store, beginning next week. If Mother and Father don't want to keep me in the house peaceably, I will simply move out and live on my own in town here," Leah showed her resolve. "I don't mind being a Protestant – that is how I believe – but I don't want to be part of a radical group."

"Under Menno, your people have been very un-radical, I would say. Henry's actions were unusual by any standards. The Mennists on the whole are very fine people, and I sometimes wish my congregation was as godly in their living as Menno's is. We don't really teach people to live like Christians, we assume they will want to do so, but most of them continue to live as the rest of the world around them, which of course means, they live like Catholics," Pastor Schmidt said solemnly, and grimaced.

"Menno makes us toe the line, or we are disciplined by the church," Leah countered. She had seen several cases where someone had over-stepped the bounds of allowable behavior and had been visited by Menno and the deacons, with the Ban following for a time, to bring the recalcitrant sheep back into the fold. "I don't think that is what churches are for, to force people to behave in ways that are strange in their society. I'm tired of being different from other girls."

"Our church also has discipline, though not to the same extent, or to the same degree of severity as yours," Pastor Schmidt warned. "People who do something that impairs the ministry of the church are not allowed to participate in communion for a time."

"In our church a person who does something that goes against the beliefs of any of the deacons gets publicly shunned by the rest of the congregation, and even his own family. This goes through all of life, until the person repents and submits to the deacons. During this time he cannot take communion, either, and no one is allowed to do busi-ness with him or speak to him, even husbands and wives cannot be together. I don't think that reflects the attitude of Jesus towards sinners at all."

Leah was amazed at her own knowledge of church affairs. Her parents had not concerned themselves very much with the politics of church life, but had simply submitted to everything that was taught by Menno and the Philips brothers. Moreover, she was amazed that her feelings had run so deeply against what her parents had taught her, that she was now willing to go her own direction, even though she was too young to legally make such a decision on her own.

"If I am to be active as a pastor's wife in the Lutheran Church, then I must be a member of the Church," Leah said with finality.

"The Baron has been visited by the Bishop of the Catholic Church, and he has demanded of him that no one be allowed to convert to another religion in his bishopric. I cannot baptize you, or we will both be held accountable. I would lose my license as a pastor, and you might lose your life," revealed Pastor Schmidt. "Henry's case has opened all the wounds of the past forty years once again, just as we thought we had gained some measure of peace between us and the Catholics. Now they are looking for anyone that turns from their church to either of the other faiths, so they have influenced the nobles to disallow any conversions at all. 'As believes the prince, so believe the people,' they say." Our Baron actually believes in a Protestant way, but he cannot afford to stand up against the machinery of the Catholic Emperor," concluded Pastor Schmidt.

"What am I supposed to do then," Leah wrung her hands in despair and looked pleadingly at the pastor.

"We must wait. You go home and continue to live as before in your parents' house, and perhaps the times will change for the better, and we will be able to carry through your wish."

Leah's countenance changed to bewilderment and frustration. She shook her head at the foibles of the leaders that controlled how she could live and believe. How would she relate to her parents now? They probably suspected her intentions. Should she try open rebellion against them, or quietly submit to their demands? That is what she was doing at present, and she would not be too suspect, if she continued. Quietly, she put her coat, shawl and gloves on, thanked the pastor for listening to her, and left.

. . .

Jake had a strange urge. After supper, he put on some clean pants and left the house. Mother wondered what that was all about, but held her peace. Jacob left the yard and went the opposite direction to that of Bad Oldesloe. Soon he was at Menno's house and knocking on the door.

"What brings you here?" said Gertrude, as she opened the door for him and helped him brush the snow off his boots and pants.

"I want to speak with Menno, if I may," he replied.

"I will see if he can come here; he was away on a preaching trip for some time before yesterday, and he has been quite tired," she explained. Jake knew he was home, because Menno had been at his house last night.

After some fussing in the other room, Gertrude appeared and stated that Menno would be there right away. Soon he appeared, somewhat disheveled of clothes, but with a freshly-washed face and freshly combed hair. His cane was the only sign of his increasing infirmity, brought on by his constant travels and deprivations.

"Please come into this room," beckoned Menno quietly. Jake followed him into the adjacent room and sat down on the bench-bed along the wall. Menno brought a chair from the kitchen and sat down opposite him.

"I want to be baptized," said Jake intently.

"What has brought you to that decision," questioned Menno. "Has Henry's martyrdom had anything to do with this?"

"Partly, but I have thought a lot about my own faith, both before and after that, and I have decided that I want to be part of the Mennist Church."

"That is very noble, Jacob. I trust that you are sincere about your faith, and that this is not just an emotional display. If it is emotional, it will not stand the test, if that should come to you, as it did to Henry."

"I am very sincere. When the Hildebrands stated last night that they wanted to be baptized, I realized that I had never taken that step. I also realize that most of the young people that are baptized in our church do so, so that they can get married, because the church doesn't marry anyone who is not baptized." Jake had the order of business figured out from the standpoint of the young people, at least.

"Everyone who desires baptism must be interviewed by me or by one of the deacons, after taking catechism classes, before they can be recommended, so it is unlikely that anyone is baptized who doesn't really believe fervently in Jesus as personal Savior. And if it is so that they can get married, it is also so that they can begin by being a Christian family right away," reasoned Menno. "Do you want to be baptized, so you can get married?" he continued with a twinkle in his eye.

"Not right away, but sometime it will happen. I would like to be baptized along with the Hildebrands, if that is possible." Jake was dangerously close to giving away his deepest personal feelings at this point.

Menno had not been totally blind during his visit to their home the night before, either, and he suspected that something might be beginning between Jacob and Heidi. *The Lord's works are wonderful,* he reasoned, *and marvelous in our eyes.* "We are planning a baptismal service in the middle of February," Menno ventured. "You will have to attend the catechism classes before then, but it is possible for you to be baptized on that Sunday."

Jake was given the information about the catechism classes and agreed to attend faithfully. Menno's expression then became very grave. "The Hildebrands will not be allowed to be baptized, even though they would like to become members of our church. The Baron has been influenced by the Bishop not to allow anyone to change religions on his estate. The Hildebrands are Catholics, and as far as the Bishop is concerned, they must remain Catholics as long as they live."

"But they believe as we do," began Jake, "why can't they follow their conscience as we do?"

"Because of Henry's actions, the whole country is up in arms against us, and the Bishop is looking for any way possible to keep his congregation from drifting away, either to the Lutherans, or to us. As long as the Baron protects us from the authorities, we seem to be safe, but he has said very emphatically, that he will not be responsible for anyone who changes his religion on his estate," Menno revealed.

The import of this decree, insofar as his relationship with Heidi was concerned, began to penetrate Jake's heart. This meant that he could not begin openly to show interest in her. It meant that he must go on alone in his relationship with God. Did he really want to do that?

"Let me think about whether I want to be baptized in February," he stated. "Perhaps I need to look at my real motivation for wanting to go through with that right now."

"Our door will always be open to you, Jacob, and when you know in your heart that God wants this of you, you will know. As for the Hildebrands, we have to trust God that time will bring healing to our broken world, and that they will be allowed to follow their conscience, too," Menno closed the conversation. He shook Jake's hand and saw him to the door. Jake put his coat and cap back on and left for home, mulling many thoughts in his muddled mind.

• • •

Heidi Hildebrand was a bundle of energy today. This was not unusual for her, but she seemed especially animated this evening. It was at her insistence that her parents had discussed the idea of converting to the Anabaptist religion. It was after their conversation in the graveyard that she began to search her own heart for why she believed as she did. Henry's brave actions had awakened in her a desire for a religious experience that was more than just traditions, ceremonies, smells and bells, but was heartfelt and personally real. She had begun to realize the force of a true belief in God, as she now knew that Henry had had. It was a faith that made a difference in his life. Not that she liked it, that he had smashed Mary. Mary was somehow special to her, someone who could understand a woman's heart and thoughts, and bring them to a holy God in special services of prayer for her devotees. It was difficult to separate what it was in her beliefs that matched her concept of God and of Jesus Christ. They seemed far away and hard to grasp. Yet, she had seen that, for Henry, at least, they were personal and close - they were life-changing. She needed more than she had, and she had begun to think that perhaps the Mennists were closer to the truth than her Church was. It was at that point she had begun to discuss these ideas with her parents.

The Hildebrands, too, had been moved by their contacts with the Mennists. Jacob Derksen was a good man, reasoned John. He worked hard and tried to learn all there was to know about hogs. He had mentioned to John that he had done quite a bit of bricklaying, but was willing to work in the hog barns, just to do his share in providing for his family and to help the Baron who had given them so much. Lizzy felt that Eva was a good woman. She was raising a fine family, and she had one special needs son among the bunch. She did not feel that Henry's actions reflected on Eva at all.

"Mother, will this dress be OK for the baptism?" Heidi called from her room. She was trying on her few dresses, thinking that one or the other looked most like a bridal dress, which Catholic girls would wear on their confirmation, and she remembered her confirmation as if it had been yesterday. *I got many gifts and cards of encouragement that day, and my godparents presented me with some valuable jewelry. None of my dresses seem to be comparable to the one I wore that day, and the jewelry will be totally inappropriate on this occasion,* she surmised. The thoughts were racing through her mind pell mell. "Oh, I don't think I have anything good enough to wear for my baptism," she lamented, just as her mother entered the room, "we're going to have to sew a new one."

"Heidi, Menno doesn't let people dress that way for their baptism," Lizzy said flatly. "Remember, if we want to be Mennists, we have to respect how they dress and not try to bring in our worldly ways."

"That's going to be hard," pouted Heidi. She loved her nice dresses and the way in which they showed off her nicely-developed feminine figure. The sacrifices of becoming a Mennist would not be easy, she thought, with her lips pursed in disappointment.

Her mother smiled knowingly, looking in Heidi's wardrobe for a dress that would be appropriate for the occasion. Unfortunately, they were all too revealing, too stylish, to be worn for a Mennist baptism.

"We will have to make you a dress, Heidi," Lizzy stated, matter-of-factly. "I will have to ask Eva if she has a pattern for something that would be suitable, and I'll have to go to Janzen's store to see if they have some cloth that will not offend our new friends."

The thought of making new friends had not really occurred to Heidi before. Couldn't she just keep her old friends? *It's my friends who keep me living as I did before my family decided to convert. Yes, it's too bad, but I will have to make new friends among the Mennists. What was that strange feeling I experienced last night at the Derksens, when I saw Jake for the first time that I can remember. Why did I seem to be drawn to him more than to Leah? She is, after all, a girl my age, with whom I could share personal thoughts. Leah could teach me how to be a good Mennist woman, or could she? Perhaps she is as fickle as I am.* Her thoughts continued to race from one topic to another.

"Let's go to Janzen's store to see about cloth," suggested Lizzy. Heidi thought that was a good idea, so she began to get ready to go out into the freshly-fallen snow with her mother.

• • •

Leah was browsing in the cloth section in Janzen's store as Heidi and Lizzy entered.

"Oh, Leah, why are you looking for cloth? Are you planning on making a new dress?" asked Heidi brightly.

"Yes, I want something that is more festive, more youthful, than what I've got," replied Leah, a bit hesitant to be speaking with Heidi.

"I've got some dresses that would fit the bill, and I won't be needing them anymore," volunteered Heidi, with a pout.

"Oh, why not?" Leah knew why, but she felt she must make conversation.

"Well, you heard that I am going to be baptized in the Mennist church sometime, and I haven't anything that Menno would approve of, to wear," explained Heidi unnecessarily.

"And I have only dresses of which he would approve, and I won't be needing them anymore, either," said Leah, with determination. "Say, I just thought of something. We are about the same size and build, and I have a new dress that I got for Christmas from Baron von Ahlefeld that would be perfect for your baptism. Why don't we just trade dresses?"

That was a new idea to Heidi and Lizzy. After a bit of discussion between them, they agreed. Leah could come over on Saturday to get Heidi's and bring her own. Both would then have time to wash everything and press them properly. That seemed to satisfy everyone.

Just then Mr. Janzen came over to where the girls and Lizzy were, looking as though he had something important to share. "Have you heard the latest word about our Baron?" he asked.

"No," they chorused, "we haven't heard anything about him."

"Father Daniel was in this morning to tell me, and later, Pastor Schmidt said the same thing, and after that, Menno came in and said the same," stated Mr. Janzen importantly. "No one is allowed to change his religion on the estate, on pain of death. The Baron says he cannot protect anyone who changes from one church to another."

The girls looked at each other, then at Lizzy. That meant that none of them could go through with their baptism.

"I was actually at Pastor Schmidt's this morning, asking about baptism into the Lutheran church, and he told me to wait, because of what the Baron had said," revealed Leah, somewhat sheepishly. "I was looking for a new dress out of rebellion."

"Maybe we were all a bit rebellious," mused Lizzy. "Well, we will all have to wait now, and see what happens. Maybe things will quiet down, and we'll be able to do so later."

The three stunned ladies moved slowly out onto the street, and after strained parting wishes, went on their ways home.

• • •

Eva had her hands full, looking after the younger children and Isaac, so she hadn't paid much attention to her two older ones' comings and goings. Jacob was at work in the Baron's hog barns. As Leah came in, she was at the kitchen stove, preparing a cabbage and turnip soup for lunch, to be eaten with some of Leah's fresh Bulki, sliced thickly, and spread with Jreiven Schmult (crackling lard).

"I must talk with you," began Leah, and continued without interruption, "I went to talk to Pastor Schmidt today, and asked to be baptized in the Lutheran Church."

Eva dropped the ladle into the soup in surprise. "Are you sure you want that?"

"I've thought a lot about it, especially since Henry was killed, and I think Lutheranism is the religion I want to follow. Besides, Hans and I will probably marry after he completes his studies to become a minister like his father, and then I would be Lutheran pastor's wife. It would be better for me to be a Lutheran, at least, if that happens." The rationale was quite clear in Leah's mind by now; she had gone over it time and again in her thoughts. "Besides, they believe in Jesus as Savior, the same as we do, and not traditions, like the Catholics. So, what's the difference, if I become a Lutheran, I am still a true Christian. Then I'll be able to wear fashionable dresses, too, and look human for a change." The last was stated with some conviction and finality.

Mother sat down on a kitchen chair, and Leah rescued the soup that was threatening to boil over. The thought that her family would split over religion had never entered Eva's mind. She had assumed that

Leah would be baptized into the Mennist Church as they had been. The curse of love had come between them! She wiped her hand in her apron and tried to wrap her mind around these new thoughts. Aron, Frederic and Miriam continued their boisterous play around her feet, while Isaac rocked to an inner melody on the bench-bed behind the table, clutching an old wooden model of a horse to his chest.

"Your Father will not be pleased to hear about this," thought Eva out loud.

"Well, the Baron has put an end to all of that," said Leah vehemently. "He has forbidden anyone from changing religions on his estate. He allows Mennists, Catholics and Lutherans to all live here and work together, but he refuses any more to allow anyone to convert from one to the other. Henry's actions have made that come on all of us."

"That will affect the Hildebrands, then, as well," the thought suddenly came to Eva.

"Yes, I met them in Janzen's store today, and they are pretty upset about it. They were planning to get baptized into the Mennist church. But, Menno had come into the store and told Mr. Janzen that the Baron had forbidden any change of religion. Mr. Janzen then told us all about it. He didn't even know that we were all there, looking for cloth to make ourselves baptismal dresses," Leah became quite animated, as she shared her experience with her mother.

Except for the noise of the children, there was nothing said over the soup and bread they were eating. Jake, Leah and Eva were deep in thought, wrestling with their inner reservations and convictions. That silence pervaded the entire evening's work, as each went about doing what they always did. This silence continued for another full day.

• • •

Jacob came home from a very hard day's work. Three sows had farrowed, and one had had trouble, so that he and John had to work very hard to save the litter and the sow. In the end, hard work and watchful eyes paid off, and all but one of the litter of 9 piglets were saved. The sow was now nursing her brood contentedly, and all would be well.

Supper was on the table, with <u>Tweiback,</u> <u>Schinkenbraten</u> (fried ham), boiled cabbage and <u>Schmauntfat</u> (cream gravy). It was winter, and only those vegetables that could be kept were available. Potatoes were only eaten on special occasions, for their first crop would not last all year, if they ate them indiscriminately. Then they wouldn't have seed for the next year, either. Cabbage could be kept in the root cellar along with the potatoes. Everyone sat down to begin, and Father signaled that grace was to be said, by looking all around the table to assure that all eyes were on him and all noise had stopped, and then bowing his head in silent thanks.

The younger ones immediately began to squabble over the various parts of the meal, either disliking the cabbage, or liking too much gravy for Mother's liking, and supper was underway. Leah and Jake ate in silence, helping when necessary to deal with the needs of their younger siblings. Mother was silent, too, listening to Father's account of his day's adventures, and of his new-found relationship with John. Instead of being only the employee and answering to John, he felt he was now becoming somewhat of a mentor to him in matters of faith. That seemed to even the playing field for them, and it made them more aware of each other's thoughts and ideas, which in turn, made them better in their work.

"John told me that the priest got wind of their thoughts of converting, and he came to visit them," Father began, "He was not happy, as you might imagine, and he spoke no end of curses on them for wanting to leave the True Church, as he called it. He assured them that they would be in purgatory forever. Then, John told me that Heidi was giving her party dress to Leah; is that true?"

Leah looked at her mother, and her mother looked at Leah knowingly. Leah began haltingly, "I wanted to be baptized in the Lutheran church this Sunday."

Father put his bread down, and looked hard at Leah. Nothing like this had ever entered his mind, and he was having a difficult time now understanding Leah's statement.

"I know you and Hans are together quite a bit, so the idea of your marrying him has entered my mind before, but I guess I always thought we would gain a son, and not lose a daughter," Jacob mused.

"You aren't losing a daughter," replied Leah testily, "Lutherans are also true Christians, like we are. They believe in salvation through Jesus Christ alone, just like we do, and they believe in following the Bible, just like we. The only difference is that they don't think we have to live like pigs to do so, ready to be slaughtered at every opportunity."

Jacob tried to understand the various parts of Leah's attack. He definitely felt it was an attack, and he was unprepared for it. He looked at Eva for direction and assurance. Eva nodded that she had already heard this from Leah, but she didn't say anything.

"We also found out that the Baron would not allow us to be baptized into another religion," began Leah, "so the Hildebrands and I will not be able to go through with what our consciences tell us to do. If you don't want me to live here anymore, I will go and live by myself in Bad Oldesloe. I begin work in Janzen's store on Monday, so I'll have my own money." Leah was becoming more defiant.

The silence of the older ones was palpable. Even the younger ones became strangely quiet and ceased their quarreling. Everyone looked from Father to Leah, then to Mother and back to Father. What was going to happen next?

Jake had sat through all of this quite quietly, deep in his own thoughts. He suddenly began to speak, "I have also talked with Menno about baptism. He told me about the Baron's decree, so that the Hildebrands could not be baptized as Mennists. That made me stop and think a bit deeper about why I wanted to be baptized at all. I have thought much about that decision, and I think I really do want to become a Mennist. But, when he told me about the Hildebrands, I decided to wait and see how things develop in the area. Perhaps the animosity will die down, and we can act on what our consciences say to us again."

Jacob, who came out of a tradition that emphasized patriarchal rule, and who had this reinforced by Menno's teachings, was nonplussed as to what to do with this newly obstreperous daughter and bewildered son. He sat with his chin on one hand, which was supported on the table by his elbow, looking at Leah thoughtfully. Truly, he could insist, with physical consequences threatened, if she did not capitulate to his demands. Something was going around in his mind, though, and that something took precedence over his first instincts. Perhaps he did not need to divide the family, if he recognized Leah's determination as legitimate. He did not want to divide the family, even though religious differences were doing that in many other families around them.

He addressed Jake first, "Yes, it would be best for you not to act in haste. Perhaps you have other, more personal reasons for waiting." His eyes began to twinkle, as he said the last part. Jake blushed, but smiled too.

He then looked at Leah, "You say you would move out, if we don't agree to your demands," began Father on a very quiet note. "I would not like to see that happen. Your mother and I would dearly love to see you become a true Mennist in your heart. You obviously believe in Jesus as the only Savior. I understand that your young mind doesn't want to accept the strict rules we live by as Mennists. It takes maturity to understand why certain rules are necessary. That will come to you over time. I hope we can learn to live together in harmony. You have several years, before Hans returns from university, so you can work at the store while living at home. That way you'll be able to save something for beginning your own home. We love you, Leah, and we don't want to see you go away without knowing that." Father was almost in tears by this time, something unfamiliar in their home. He looked at Leah with pleading in his eyes, then at Mother, who definitely had tears in hers.

Leah leapt from her place and threw her arms around her father's neck. "Oh, thank you for understanding, Father," she sobbed. "I will be happy to live with you and see what God will do."

# Chapter Ten

The winter evening drew its shutters and turned off all its lights. No lingering sunlight penetrated the fog that covered a vast area of northern Germany. Bad Oldesloe, with its neighboring village of Wuestenfelde, were held in its icy vapor, as figures bundled themselves against the cutting cold, but continued walking in spite of it. Because no one could see very far ahead, no one knew that there were others about that evening. All, however, were heading toward a central place, the bare old linden tree in the center of Bad Oldesloe. Nearby was the Kurhaus, where the warm mineral waters that gave Bad Oldesloe its name were made available for a high price to people for their aches and pains. Lights penetrated the fog from its large windows, and there seemed to be some activity going on in the large atrium that made up the front hall. But that would be for noble or rich folk, the peasant community were generally satisfied to be at home by a warm hearth with their families on a night like tonight.

The four figures, however, were young, and they were hopeful in meeting their loved one under the linden tree. Had it been summertime, the leaves of the tree would have shrouded the lovers from all view, but now, in wintertime, the bare branches provided little privacy.

The fog, however, allowed no visibility to outsiders, so the lovers would be able to meet in complete privacy in this public place.

Hans Schmidt and Heidi Hildebrand had the shortest distance to walk, but they came from opposite ends of Bad Oldesloe, so were completely unaware of each other. Jake and Leah had three kilometres to walk, but they were also unaware of each other, as they had left the house at different times. The fog seemed not only to impair visibility, but it seemed also to deaden any sound that footfalls might be making.

As each neared the tree, however, it became obvious that this trysting place was not just that for one couple, but for two. All four arrived in very close succession, and when they pulled back their heavy winter hoods, each was able to recognize the others.

"Well, it looks as though it wasn't just Jacob and me that wanted to meet tonight," said Heidi cheerfully. She was the talkative one of the group, so she was also the first to speak up.

"Leah and I have been meeting here quite regularly," chimed in Hans, who was also never at a loss for words.

"I think our reason for meeting is pretty much the same for both couples," said Leah, "so I think it won't hurt, if we all stay together. Maybe it will be warmer anyway, if we aren't all alone."

"I don't think it would matter, if we went to the Gasthaus on an evening like this. There won't be any drunks there tonight, so we would probably have the place to ourselves. Did anyone bring any money along, so we can at least buy one drink to make our visit legal?" Jake was always the practical one, and he had a suitable solution for their meeting this evening. He checked and found he had some change, and Hans also had some. Everyone agreed, so off they went.

As suspected, there were no customers in the Gasthaus. Fritz, the innkeeper, was the only person there, and he was drying glasses behind the bar. The group found a suitable table, with a corner bench behind it and a couple of chairs in front. A fireplace with warm, glowing coals was cheerily close. Jacob and Heidi slid in behind the table onto the bench, while Leah and Hans took the chairs in front.

"What will we drink tonight?" asked Hans, with a twinkle in his eye, "I'm having some nice smooth red wine."

"I think I'll have some, too," said Leah, softly, "but I'll have mine with mineral water, please." She knew that her parents only drank wine on special occasions, such as Christmas, when the Baron provided them with it. Otherwise, it was usually homemade ale – a type of beer without hops to smooth its flavour – so it was somewhat bitter.

"I'll have a beer," said Jacob, and Heidi decided she, too, would have red wine, mixed with mineral water.

As Fritz prepared their drinks, the young people settled themselves comfortably and began to make small talk. Once the drinks arrived and were distributed, they began to grapple with the issues they were facing.

"It's not fair," exploded Heidi, "we should be able to follow our consciences and not have anyone telling us what we may or may not believe."

"You're right," droned Leah, somewhat weary of thinking about her binding situation.

The men didn't seem as concerned as the young ladies were about this, as neither had intentions of changing religions. They were, however, concerned that their respective partners were hampered in their desire to change religious affiliations. Most especially, they were wondering what the attitude of their partner was to the limitation that had been placed on their plans. Since both women had expressed dismay at the prospects, both men were relieved to know that their partner was still interested in them, even if they couldn't change religions to the one of their lover.

"We could run away and elope," suggested Heidi brightly. She seemed to have gotten over her loss of Henry very quickly, thought Jacob, but he was glad for her attention to him. Then he thought of the fact that Henry and Heidi had only expressed interest in each other quite recently, so perhaps their relationship had not become very deep and personal.

"There's no place to go," countered Jacob dryly, "and we wouldn't have anything to live on, if there were." Jacob was not one to be easily led astray from his carefully thought out plans. "I have just begun to learn the skills of carpentry, and I need to work at it for a few years, before I strike out on my own. I think we just have to wait and hope that things will calm down, and we'll be ignored."

"I want to get away to study anyway, so there is no thought of other change of any kind right now," said Hans, "we'll just have to continue with our plans and hope that things will settle down in the meantime." Hans was also gratified that Leah seemed to be just as interested in him now as she was before the decree that forbade her becoming a Lutheran, so she could be married to a Lutheran pastor.

"Yes, you get to go away and leave us here in boredom and disgrace," lamented Leah.

"You're not in disgrace, Leah," Jake chimed in, "Mother and Father have been very loving and gracious about this whole thing, I think."

"Yes, I must admit that I thought they would be much more violently against what I wanted, but they have been most accommodating. I can even stay at home while working in the store. Menno, however, won't be nearly as easy to get away from, and he finds out everything about those he thinks are his flock." Leah's bitterness couldn't be hidden. She knew she was going against her parents' wishes, which included Menno's wishes, but she loved Hans, and she would not be dissuaded from becoming a Lutheran. *I am a Lutheran in my heart,* she reasoned, and needed to be able to express it.

"I'm the one who has to make the biggest change," began Heidi. "You all know that I have been a devout Catholic, and my family has also been very devout. Not everyone in our church is that devoted. For some, it is just a tradition to be followed generation after generation. For some, it seems to be a fire escape from hell, to be taken at the last minute through special rites the priest performs on the deathbed. I even bought an indulgence that was supposed to provide me with eternal salvation and get my grandmother out of 100,000 years of purgatory.

Now I think this is all silly. God seems to have gotten a hold on my life, and He has also gotten a hold on my parents. Then, the Baron decides to protect the churches and not allow any conversions in his estate. That sort of makes my family's plans to be baptized in the Mennist Church a thing of the past. Father Daniel is gloating every time he sees me or my parents. I think he is just counting the ducats he will receive from us, if we remain in the church."

"Remember, you won't be able to wear your nice clothing any more, if you become a Mennist," reminded Leah, who was envious of Heidi's fashionable dresses, shoes and bonnets. "All I ever get to wear are old-fashioned granny dresses, with dark shawls."

"You know that isn't true," said Jake from behind his beer froth. "Your dresses are actually quite pretty, and you would make any dress pretty, just by wearing it, anyway." Jake had never been so complimentary to his sister, and she turned a brilliant scarlet on hearing this statement from him.

"Oh, ah, but . . ." Leah stammered, but found no words to complete her retort. Hans, ever quick to rescue a situation, put his arm around her and gave her a good squeeze around the shoulders. Theirs was not a relationship that included anything more than a hug and an occasional kiss, and his action was very reassuring to Leah right then.

"So, what are we ladies-in-waiting going to do for excitement, when Hans is gone, and Jake gets more involved in learning the skills of carpentry?" asked Heidi, a bit impudently. "It looks as though we will be spending lots of quiet evenings at home alone from now on. I suppose I'll have to take up knitting or crocheting, perhaps I can make lace doilies." Her tone changed from frivolity to downright sarcasm.

"Do we really want to convert?" Leah's question took a little while to sink in. "It's only we girls that are converting; you men are staying right where you have always been. Is conversion only a thing that women do? What is the real purpose of converting, anyway? Is it because we believe something now that we didn't before, or is it just because we have men to go after, and this is the only way we see to get one?" She had obviously been doing a bit of thinking, and she had realized an important ingredient of religious expression.

There was silence for some time, as they all stared into the glasses before them and sought answers to these deep questions in the fiery liquid at the bottom. *Why do we believe? What is the real purpose for religion? Why are there different approaches to finding God? Which one is right?* Each one wrestled quietly with Leah's question, that had uncovered the very personal nature of religious faith. At that moment, they began to hear sounds of music coming from the Kurhaus.

• • •

"Why do we have to have a divided family," Eva couldn't get the idea out of her mind. "Leah wants to become a Lutheran, so she can marry Hans, and Jake is interested in a Catholic girl, who isn't allowed to convert, so he could marry her." To a mother, especially a Mennist mother, the question of a marriage partner for their maturing children was of gravest importance.

"Now, don't fret, Eva, you know that God will help all things to work out for good, because we love Him and want His will. Satan will always throw things in the way, but in the end, God will triumph in both Leah's and Jake's lives." Jacob's faith held firmly to God's sovereignty in their lives; he had seen it at work in the many times they were fleeing from persecution and were miraculously spared.

Eva's deepest thoughts, on the other hand, revolved around the fact that they had constantly to flee from impending danger. *God's protection came, often just in the nick of time, but why couldn't He just have protected us in such a way, that there was no danger to flee from? I'm tired of the life that we chose early in our marriage, not tired of being a Mennist, but tired of the constant barrage of criticism and the everlasting attempts of the church to find us and exterminate us. I am thankful for the Baron's protection, but how long will he be able to resist the overpowering tradition that keeps the Emperor and the church in league against us? And the Lutherans, they consider the Mennists to be heretics, too, because we rejected infant baptism. When will my family finally live in peace and security, without constant threat of attack or turning from what we believe? Have we not taught our children well enough? Am I a failure as a mother?*

Jacob moved behind the rocking chair in which Eva was sitting, placed his hands on her shoulders and squeezed her neck, to assure her of his love and support. He didn't know what to say to comfort her, or to assure her of her worth and success. For a few moments their combined silence seemed to permeate the air in their living room. Only the sound of the fire on the hearth could be heard. Jacob tended to meditate for some time, before giving words to his thoughts. Eva sobbed quietly into her apron.

Jacob began with some difficulty, "I don't know if this is connected with what we are facing, my dear, but today the Baron came to the hog barn and asked to speak to me personally. He said that he is considering building a new barn for the pigs, and to add another for his cattle and horses, and he is looking for a bricklayer with experience. He had heard that this is what I did for many years, so he wondered whether I could head up that building project."

"What did you tell him?" asked Eva incredulously.

"I told him that I would consider it, but lacked experience in leading people in the job. I have always worked under a master bricklayer, never on my own. I understand the skills of building well enough, but will I be able to lead others in such a big job?" Jacob was never one to overreach his own limitations. "He said that, if I take the job, he would provide us with a bigger and better house closer to his estate buildings, where the barns are to be built."

"You can certainly lead people. You were elected a deacon in our congregation, weren't you?" Eva saw no limitations in anyone except herself. Jacob thought about that for a while, for he had not connected the one type of leadership with the other. He moved back to his comfortable chair and stared at the floor for some time before speaking.

"As I was saying, I don't know how this will affect our other issues right now. It would put all of us closer to our workplace, which would be a great benefit to our family life. Jake could easily get to his carpentry shop, and Leah could easily get to the store. You would have more contacts in Bad Oldesloe than you can have here in Wuestenfelde, and that might help you in looking after Isaac. I would be quite close to the barns that we would start to build quite soon, as soon as the frost leaves the ground this spring." Jacob was gaining momentum, as he saw the benefits of taking on this responsibility. "So, do you think I should accept the job and the move?"

"I think it would be good for all of us. Perhaps we could also get some special schooling for Isaac, if we were in Bad Oldesloe. I've heard that there is a Dorfschwester in the Lutheran church there, who takes on children with special needs and gives them practical instruction to help them to be able to live independently." It was Eva's turn to become excited now, and her words and ideas tumbled out tumultuously.

"I wonder what Menno will say to this proposal," reflected Jacob, "he depends on me, especially when he is travelling."

"His health is not good enough to be travelling, and Gertrude's is fading very quickly. I don't think she will be with us much longer," responded Eva.

"You're right, I guess we could continue to be active in the congregation, even though we might live further away from where we meet for services. We are going to be building a church soon, too, and that could involve some more bricklaying. Oh, if both start at the same time, we are going to be very busy," rambled Jacob.

"Still, I do believe God wants me to take the bricklaying job, rather than stay in the hog barn," Jacob continued, after thinking for a while. "I'll tell the Baron tomorrow that I'll accept the job. For now, however, would you care to go with me for a walk in the fog? The children are either out or asleep, so we could spend a quiet evening outside."

• • •

Baron Bartholomew von Ahlefeld had an important visitor. Adolf, the Duke of Holstein-Gottorp, had arrived with several attendants and would be spending the night at the estate with the Baron. This was a singular honor for the Baron, for though he owned extensive tracts of land within Holstein, he was not a high-ranking nobleman. The Duke, on the other hand, was a brother to the Danish King, and quite high in the German hierarchy of noblemen, as evidenced by his title of Duke. The attendants were left together with the Baron's staff, to sort out where the horses should be stabled, the carriage stored under roof, and the baggage brought to the proper rooms in the estate buildings. Meanwhile, the Duke and the Baron strolled toward the house, chatting about the trip from Gottorp Castle to Altfresenburg, the manor where the Baron lived. The weather had turned rather bitter, with the thick impenetrable fog blanketing the entire region from the North Sea and Baltic Sea down to Hamburg.

After taking the Duke's heavy winter cloak and showing him to a comfortable chair in the parlor, the Baron proceeded to pour a couple of glasses of wine, and then offered one to his guest, while he swirled his wine around and sniffed the bouquet of the quality product. As they sat, they looked at each other as friends do, who have not seen each other for some time.

"This is a great surprise, Duke Holstein-Gottorp, and a great honor, to have you come to visit me," began the Baron, showing his deference to his superior.

"Bartholomew, let's skip the formalities, please, I'm Adolf to you," responded the Duke, "after all, we've been friends for years." This meant, of course, that from there on, they would use the familiar instead of the formal in their conversation, and the whole grammatical construction of each sentence would reflect this familiarity in their relationship. "I didn't know whether your visit meant something sinister, or something good," laughed Bartholomew more easily.

"There are business items, to be sure, but most importantly, I want to see firsthand what your Mennists are doing for you on your estate," replied Adolf quite candidly.

"We can visit some of the various agricultural and building operations in which the Mennists are involved tomorrow, but we'll have to hope the fog clears, before we can see where most of them live and other things connected with their being here." The Baron was now much more at ease, but he still wondered what the 'business items' were that brought his friend to his estate. Realizing that Adolf was a staunch Lutheran kept Bartholomew's mind jumping from one possibility to another, insofar as 'business items' might be concerned. Perhaps it would be a good time to change the subject.

"The Emperor hasn't been agitating very much recently," he ventured.

"Actually, that touches close to why I came," Adolf was surprised at Bartholomew's candor in commenting on such a volatile subject. "I've heard that he has resigned as Emperor, and has entered a monastery in Spain. His health is not too good, I believe, but I think he is just tired of the religious fighting that has plagued his whole reign. You know how those Hapsburgs are, always defending the faith, regardless of against whom they have to fight, even their own. He has avoided fighting the true foe, who is Suleiman the Magnificent, who is determined to bring Islam to Europe, and has tried a couple of times to capture Vienna. He has already held Buda and Pest for some time, but he's not satisfied with Hungary, he wants the rest of Europe. I guess he thinks that Charles Martel's victory over the Moors in Tours can be revenged from another direction. My brother and others in Scandinavia have embraced Lutheranism and are lined up against the empire's Catholic leaders. I am one of them, too. You helped the Dutch in their fight for independence from him, so you also show tendencies of anti-imperialism."

The Duke had rambled on at length about the situation in Europe, and Bartholomew sat, sipping slowly on his Spanish wine. The final statement jarred his mind from its personal reveries. "Yes, I must confess that I don't approve of many of the imperial policies. It seems that they all revolve around the church's need to have German funds for an Italian Pope's wishes," added Bartholomew.

Now it was Adolf's turn to sip his Spanish wine and contemplate. Batholomew broke into his thoughts, "My taking the Mennists onto my estate had a lot to do with that dissatisfaction," he began. "Of course, the plague had decimated my subjects, so there was a need to import workers and settlers, in order to do the work on the estate, but also to satisfy the plans I have for this estate."

At that moment, Bartholomew's wife entered the room, curtsied charmingly to the Duke, and invited the men into the dining room for supper. The men rose from their chairs as she entered the room, and followed, as she led them to the table.

"What a wonderful meal," praised Adolf, I haven't had such fresh veal for a long time, and those potatoes, they are a special treat. I'll have to have some seedlings planted in spring myself; they surely do taste good with the meat and gravy, don't they?"

"Yes, I was offered some by a prince in Holland and took some home with me to plant. They produced a good crop last year. I was able to give some seedlings to each of my peasant families this year," replied Bartholomew, "rather progressive of me, don't you think? They do originate in the New World, you know. It appears that Pizarro got them from the Incas and brought them back to Spain. From there they have been distributed over more and more of Europe." The Duke seemed impressed that he should be served Inca delicacies in northern Germany.

As supper concluded with an apple cobbler for dessert, Bartholomew announced, "I have brought a troupe of musicians in to play at the Kurhaus this evening. Would you like to accompany us to hear them?"

# Chapter Eleven

The performance of the group had just begun; the musicians were playing a rousing march as their introductory piece. The group was made up of a treble viol, played the way modern violins are played, and a viola da gamba, played upright on the lap, plus a wooden transverse flute and a lute, with portative organ accompaniment. The somewhat nasal sound carried well into the foggy night. As the foursome emerged from the Gasthaus, they could see through the large windows of the Kurhaus that a small crowd had gathered to hear the group. Seemingly drawn as by a magnet, they slipped into the back row of chairs and began to listen. Others kept coming, as well. Between the first piece and the next the Baron, together with his wife and the Duke, were announced, and could be seen moving toward the front row, where special seats had been arranged for them where they could best hear and see.

As the slow Ländler was being played next, the eyes of the small group in the rear went over the details of the room in which they found themselves. Prominently hanging from the ceiling by chains were two huge crystal chandeliers, with great candles burning warmly against the cold outside, their flames scintillating from the facets of the various prisms hanging among the candles. The walls were paneled in wood, and there were several paintings of long-forgotten local noblemen hanging on the walls. The ceiling was plastered in white stucco, with moldings to give it a more cultured effect. The floor was laid in great slabs of stone, with grey grouting between. A rug runner ran down the middle, between two groups of chairs set up in a semi-circle for best views of the performers. The Baron and his wife rose at the sound of the music, and proceeded to demonstrate the slow and graceful movements of the old country Ländler dance. Three other couples, all prominent business people in town, joined them. Heidi and Leah were fascinated by the evening dresses the ladies were wearing, while Jake and Hans kept their eyes on the instrumentalists, themselves fascinated by the technique displayed by each performer and the distinct sounds each instrument made in various registers.

As each one became lost in his or her own world of thought and introspection, none noticed others entering the hall, until it was totally filled. Piece after piece was played, enthralling all who attended. Some were simply performance pieces, others were dance music to which various ones responded with varying degrees of aptitude. The Duke escorted the Baron's wife in one of these dances. Jacob and Leah had never learned to dance, so they were too afraid to step forward. Besides, none of them had dressed to go to a concert; their business had been totally different. They had landed in the performance more or less by accident.

As the last piece was announced, the group seemed to acknowledge their inappropriate presence in the hall and prepared to leave. Unknown to them, Jacob and Eva, who had stumbled upon the concert just as it was ending and were standing near the door, were also preparing to leave.

"I see we had company," said Hans, as he spied an older couple leaving the building just ahead of their group, and then another, and finally, his own parents. Hans greeted his parents formally, acknowledging that they had shared a wonderful experience. Heidi was jubilant that her parents had been able to hear the group and bubbled, as she talked with them about it. Leah was suddenly afraid that she had done something that would find reproof from her father. Jake was seemingly unperturbed.

"If they were also listening, then I think we can easily be excused for having listened ourselves," he reasoned.

"It was certainly a lovely concert," added Heidi, "I haven't heard a group that good for a long time. Very interesting mix of instruments, too. Although they were so different, each contributed just the right sound to make the whole sound interesting."

The young people parted with statements that they would simply have to wait out the time of separation and see what would be possible later, to get them back together. Hans was leaving the next morning for university. Jake and Leah hurried and caught up to their parents, and together, the group made their way back to Wuestenfelde. On the way, Jacob told his daughter and now oldest son of the proposed job change and of their moving plans. This now became the focus of their discussion and the crux of their plans for the future.

• • •

As the Hildebrands and Heidi walked through Bad Oldesloe to their home, the discussion drifted slowly from the concert to what the young people had decided about their future. Heidi, ever impetuous, was obviously going to find her situation one of impatience and frustration. She had set her heart on an early marriage to Jake, and she was not happy now that they would have to wait to convert to the Mennist church, in order to get married.

"Jacob thinks that he has to spend a couple of years working in the carpentry shop, before he is able to consider marriage and a family," pouted Heidi, "so he thinks that having a time of reflection and waiting is just fine. What am I going to do in the meantime, knit baby clothes and take up crocheting or lace making? This is going to be very boring." There didn't seem to be much in the way of spiritual passion in her voice or expressions, so her parents wondered what it was that had motivated her thoughts of conversion.

"I thought we were converting, because we felt that the Mennist teachings were the right ones, not because you wanted to get married," probed her father.

"Yes, that's true, but the Mennists won't let a couple marry, unless both are members of their church. Jacob wants to be baptized, too, and now he has put that off, until we can do it together. The Baron's decree has just ruined everything for us all," continued Heidi in her pouting frame of mind.

"Now, now, Heidi, we will all have to wait until it is safe for us to join the Mennist church," remonstrated Lizzy, "In the meantime, we'll find something that you can do. Perhaps you want to learn to work with children or teach school? We could send you somewhere to learn one of those occupations."

"I suppose that would be best, since I couldn't stand being at home all the time, and I couldn't see myself working in a store, like Leah." Heidi was quite adamant in her indecision.

"We will continue to read Menno's teachings, and in that way we'll be better prepared, when we are able to be baptized," said John. "Jake, I hear, is reading his new Bible pretty faithfully, so maybe you can get together for Bible reading, and that will help prepare you for what comes later, too."

This seemed to be a good solution to all of them, and they reached their house just then, so all went in and prepared for bed.

• • •

The Schmidts walked in silence for a short distance, absorbed in the beauty of the concert they had heard.

"I leave tomorrow morning for Wittenberg," began Hans. "I'm going to miss you and Leah a lot, but I know this is what I should do."

"It is always difficult to leave home for the first time for an extended time," replied Mrs. Schmidt. "We will also miss you, but you will write, won't you? Your brothers are terrible at communicating, but your sister occasionally writes from Cologne. And maybe you'll even come home during holidays?" Her mother's heart was torn for her youngest, just as it had been for each of the older children, when they left home.

"You will have plenty to occupy your time at the university," continued Pastor Schmidt. "There is a great deal of reading to do, and you will have to write many dissertations before you graduate as a pastor."

"I look forward to that. I guess studying comes naturally to me, and I love to learn. I look forward to getting into the theological teachings that differentiate our faith from that of the Catholics and the Mennists," Hans was optimistic that he would be able to figure out what was real from what was merely tradition. "I guess it all boils down to this: On what do we base our beliefs, the Bible, or Church tradition?"

"You have landed exactly on the spot where Luther found out that there is a vast difference," expounded the Pastor. "We Lutherans and the Mennists agree on this, for certain: The Bible is and must be the basis of every aspect of our faith. Luther's maxim rings in my mind: 'sola scriptura, sola fide, sola gratia, solus Christus, soli Deo gloria.'"

"Still, I will miss Leah very much. She's such a gem, and I will be happy to come back to see her as often as possible, too." Hans was beginning to feel the pangs of separation already. "I suppose it is good that we will be separated. People say that absence makes the heart grow fonder, but I sincerely doubt that. I think love grows, when two people are together a lot, and cools when they are separated for long times. I'm worried she may find someone among the Mennists, that will suit her family more than I do, and give in to her parents' wishes to marry him."

"If that happens, then you would be better off not having her in the first place," Mrs. Schmidt observed. "You think you love her now, and it is probably true love, but remember, it does hinge on whether she converts to our religion."

"I've thought about that, too," Hans replied. "If I want to be a Lutheran pastor, I would want her to be my helper, not my competition. I doubt that this separation will make her change her mind, so I'm hopeful that my time away will deepen our relationship, both with each other and with God."

"Both are important, if you want to be an effective minister of the gospel," reflected Pastor Schmidt. They entered the manse and prepared for bed. Tomorrow would provide plenty of excitement.

• • •

The Baron and the Duke, after profuse thanks to the musicians and to the prominent citizens of the town, also made their way out and back to the great estate mansion. Bundled against the foggy coolness, they did not take time to discuss anything while their carriage brought them under the roof in front of the door, where they could dismount in relative dryness and proceed inside, where the servants had a roaring fire started in the fireplace. Taking off their long heavy overcoats and giving them to the butler to put away, they walked into the parlor, where another fireplace blazed warmly.

"I'm happy that you were able to be here for that fine concert," began Bartholomew, pouring each of them a small glass of cherry *schnapps* that had been distilled on the estate. Together they toasted each other's success, and sat down on comfortable chairs across from each other, with the fire burning invitingly between them. Soon both eyes seemed bored into the blue flames near the pieces of beech wood that were giving off welcome heat and tantalizing flickers of light. Each pondered the probable thoughts of the other.

The Duke was wearing his long close-fitting stockings, with brightly striped bloomers and a tight-fitting black vest with shiny metal buttons and chains. He had shoes with pointed toes that came well beyond his actual feet. The Baron wore somewhat the same type of clothing as his peasants, though of much better quality. Depicting your rank through your clothes was very important to the nobility.

"With the Emperor now in a monastery and his brother Ferdinand now in control in this area, we will have to watch quite carefully what happens," Adolf broached the subject he wanted to discuss with Bartholomew. "We may have to supply some troops for him, because he is thinking of attacking Suleiman, or at least to defend Vienna against the Turks. Do you have a standing army that you could volunteer? I don't imagine the Mennists, with their confounded ideas about pacifism, would be of much help to you there."

"I have very few soldiers, actually," replied Bartholomew, "and none, really, that are trained and ready for battle. When I was in Holland, I commanded a Dutch regiment. Yes, the Mennists will not fight in any army; they would rather die at the stake than give up their belief that it is wrong to take up the sword. There wouldn't be any point in trying to recruit anyone out of their group."

"Hmm, then I will have to get some from another nobleman. Could you be prepared to send a hundred men, though?" requested Adolf.

"I doubt that I could get fifty from my whole estate, and they would not be reliable soldiers, but out-of-shape Catholic peasants who would have to leave their field jobs to go to war," Bartholomew grimaced at his weakened state. "Most of my fighting men died in the plague, remember? That's why I brought the Mennists in to till my fields and look after my livestock. My few Lutherans are mostly businessmen, and we need to keep their shops open."

As the Baron described the composition of his estate, the Duke nodded, seeming to understand his friend's predicament. "Still, we need to have whatever you can provide, as I am responsible for a fairly large army to send to Vienna." The Baron could scarcely hide his indignation at what his friend was demanding. Still, he was his superior, so he nodded his tacit agreement. "Now, I asked you to forbid anyone from converting from one religion to another; have you done what is necessary about that? Have you contacted the various religious leaders in your estate?" the Duke went on with his questions.

"Yes, I have done that," Bartholomew grimaced again, for it was not what he had wanted for his people. His progressive nature leaned toward allowing religious freedom to those who lived in his care. "All the leaders have assured me that they are taking appropriate steps to inform their people, and then enforce discipline among their parishioners."

"I understand that there were some who had decided to convert, though, have they gone through with their plans and gotten baptized in the other churches?" Adolf continued his questioning.

"No baptisms have taken place on my estate at all since then," replied the Baron sadly, "not even children."

"It is better that we don't allow conversion, so that some measure of peace can be maintained in the realm. We already have enough problems trying to get our Catholics and our Lutherans to live together in some form of harmony, and now the Mennists are becoming a menace to both religions," continued the Duke. "If war broke out between all of them now, it would be a terrible thing, and we would lose so many of all the groups, that it would be difficult to rebuild the population at all. I really would appreciate it, if you would send the Mennists away from our duchy." The Duke was unaware that his fears foreshadowed a cataclysm that was to come in a later generation. "You must enforce that decree with stern reality, or you will pay an awful price in the future."

Bartholomew agreed and promised to see that no conversions took place. He knew of two cases where this was contemplated – the Hildebrands and Leah – and he believed he could handle both of them by simply going to the people concerned and emphasizing the importance of not doing anything rash at this time. It was distasteful, but, as bitter medicine, it had to be swallowed to cure the problems of the realm. "I will take care of those who contemplate conversion, but I don't think I can send the Mennists away. First of all, they are no menace to anyone; secondly, I need them to build up my estate again, and thirdly, I believe they have some elements of truth that our other religions don't possess. I have remained a Catholic in name only, my leanings are definitely Protestant, and I believe that Menno is closer to the Bible than either the Pope or Luther."

The Duke, who was a staunch Lutheran, was somewhat aghast at the Baron's forthrightness, but he held his peace. The Baron was too good an ally to antagonize. He needed his support for the war against the Turks and for adding to his own revenues through the dues of serfdom owing him from his inferior nobleman.

The next day began warmer, and the fog had lifted, so the Baron took the Duke on a trip around his estate, showing him the various activities that took place there. They stopped first at the hog barn, where several hundred pigs were kept. Bartholomew introduced the Duke to John Hildebrand and Jacob, who were in charge of the hog operation, then they went to the carpentry shop, where they met Abe Voth and his crew, including Jake. A drive down various streets in Bad Oldesloe and down the road to Wuestenfelde helped the Duke to understand what the situation was, where the Mennists, as well as Lutherans, had found refuge from the Emperor on the Fresenburg Estate. He admired the Baron's progressive approaches, and he wondered how it could be possible that three groups with different religions could live side by side without rancor.

Later, as they paused for a drink at the mansion, the Duke asked, "Do you think the Mennists will build a church here, with Menno's health failing and a decree that no one may convert to join them?"

"Yes, I think so. Most of them have large families, large enough to populate an estate like mine quite soon, actually, as the children grow up and have their own families," said the Baron. "I have found them to be excellent workers and very responsible in their dealings with me and with others in the area. They come with experience that I can use. One of the men in the hog barn, for instance, has experience in bricklaying, gathered in various places where they fled, so I have asked him to head up the building of my new hog barn in spring, and then a barn for my other livestock. His son is apprenticing in the carpentry shop;

you met him there. We have quality people here, who will give us no trouble. The incident where one of them went too far and destroyed Catholic Church property is a one-of-a-kind one, which I doubt will ever be repeated again here. Someone just went off his mind, I think, to do that." Bartholomew considered it none of the Duke's business that the two men he had pointed out as fine examples of Mennists on his estate were actually the family of the condemned man.

"Well, if I get fifty of your people to come to fight at Vienna, you'll have to depend even more on the Mennists to carry the load on your estate. I notice that you also gave each of them a plot of their own land to farm for their own use; how is that going to work out for you, if the others leave their plots?" the Duke asked.

"The Mennists are not only good workers in my fields and theirs, they care for others in the community, too. They have already taken charge of looking after the elderly and widows, caring for their plots of land along with theirs, so that these people can also continue to live decently," replied the Baron, leaving the Duke shaking his head in wonder at the unmistakable gold mine he had inherited with the Mennists in his realm.

# Chapter Twelve

Jake worked hard at the carpentry shop. He knew no other way to apply himself, except with everything he had in him. Every new skill to be learned was studied from every possible angle, so as to understand it fully, in order to be applied to whatever he was building at the time. When Abe Voth gave him any plans for some new object to be made, he took them home with him and laid them out on the kitchen table and studied them by candlelight in the evening. Jacob, his father, was often found bent over the plans, as well, for he had an interest in anything to do with construction, either buildings or objects of use.

"Carpentry is a wonderful trade," blurted Jake with uncharacteristic zeal. "I love working with wood. It feels so good in the hand, and it can be worked into such beautiful things. I loved the hardwood carvings in the Kurhaus. They were so exquisitely done, almost as though they had come to life. I love the different smells of the various woods; there is a distinction between the smell of oak, or beech, or cedar, or pine that is wonderful."

"Should we get some wood carving tools?" asked Father. "I think I could enjoy doing some of that, too."

"That would be good," exclaimed Jake. "It would go well with the basic carpentry skills I am learning in the Baron's shop, and it would be fun to learn how to bring out the things I see in a piece of wood, when I hold it in my hand. Is there anyone that could teach us the basic skills?"

"I believe there is someone in Bad Oldesloe. I will ask. When we move in spring, we could also use some things to help decorate our new house," suggested Father.

"Why won't Menno allow us to decorate our church?" Jake turned the conversation to something he had been wondering about. Having seen the beauty of the Kurhaus, he compared it to the absolute plainness of their church. It seemed to him that art was a necessary part of life, but Menno obviously disapproved of it in any form in church.

"People tend to worship idols in any form," began Father, "everything can be made into an idol, and any artwork can be worshiped instead of the Creator of all beauty."

"But we don't have to. No one was worshiping the chandeliers in the Kurhaus, or the pictures on the wall."

"No, but remember, Henry was disturbed by the fact that the priest in the Catholic Church prays to the image of Mary. This is idolatry in church, we think. We must stay as far from it as possible, so Menno has said that it is better not to have anything that might tempt someone to worship it. That's also why we don't have instruments in the church, or sing in parts, as that brings out the worldly feelings in people. The simpler we can worship God, the better." Jacob was surprised at how much he could explain to his son. Perhaps his being elected a deacon had given him special insights he could now share with others.

"I can see that for church, perhaps, but what about in the home?" continued Jake.

"Idolatry can occur anywhere and with anything that we put in place of God," stated Jacob with authority.

"But, we don't have to worship a figure, just because it represents something in nature, or anything else, for that matter. It is just that, a representation of something we think of or see around us, it is beauty of form," argued Jake.

"When we build the new church, it would be nice to have decorated pews to sit in, rather than those hard benches we now have," continued Jake. "I've seen them in some churches, and I think they look much more like something that honors God, than those simple benches we have. They don't even have backs to them."

"Worshiping God is not done for comfort, Jacob, it is better that we are not comfortable when we come before our holy God," reflected Jacob. "Besides, if there are no backs on the benches, no one goes to sleep during the sermon, either."

"What about when Widow Thiessen nearly fell off the bench last week?" countered Jake. "If the ladies beside her hadn't caught her, she would have. As it was, I could hear her sleepy breathing from over on our side of the church."

The deacon wasn't pleased at the turn of the conversation. "Let's just leave things as they are," he stated with finality. Both men smiled and nodded their heads at this.

"By the way, have you thought any more about getting baptized in our church," asked Father, hoping to break the tension.

"I'm not sure what to do. I wanted to be baptized together with the Hildebrands, but since the Baron has decreed that they can't change from the Catholic Church, I don't know what I want to do."

"Do you want to be baptized, or do you want to be married? It seems to me that there is more connection to a wedding here than to your faith, if you are waiting for the Hildebrands." chuckled Father.

"True, it does seem that way, but remember, I haven't said anything about changing religions, it was Heidi and her parents that wanted that. It all sort of happened at the same time, though, so I guess I can't blame you for seeing it all as one big activity," replied Jake, also smiling. "I will have to make up my mind, I guess, whether to go ahead with baptism on my own, or wait for things to calm down, so we can do it together. I only know that Heidi is getting more impatient every day." His expression had changed to one of seriousness and contemplation.

"We have to act on spiritual impulses when they are with us, or God will walk away and not bother us anymore about it. He does not force Himself on us, but waits for us to respond to His quiet voice within," Father philosophized.

"Yes, you're right, I will talk to Menno again about this matter. It is too late for the time we had set at first, that will happen on Sunday for the other people that were waiting," said Jake.

• • •

Hans was a whirlwind of activity. The final things needed to be packed into his bags, and space was becoming a bit of a problem. With a great effort, he closed the final bag and set it with the others that were standing by the door of the manse, ready for the carriage that would take him to Lübeck, where he could catch another carriage going toward Wittenberg. He wasn't sure how many changes he would have to make to get to university, but he would be able to find out from the carriage driver, where he had to go to catch the next one going in the direction he was going.

Pastor Schmidt was concerned that his son needed to take so much money with him, but there was no other way to handle that problem than to take the coinage necessary for his education. Gold and silver coins had to be weighed out and counted, to make sure there was enough to cover Hans's expenses.

Mrs. Schmidt's concern was that her son had all he would need to look after himself. How would he wash his clothes, and who would trim his hair? These seemed to be major issues to her, and her comments and questions seemed to rotate between one or the other of those categories. Hans did not know any answers to these, except to say that other students had survived at Wittenberg for a number of years, so he thought he could, too.

Just before the carriage came to pick him up, everything seemed to be ready to go. Farewells were hopeful, tearful, and stoic, all at the same time, but after loading the bags, Hans climbed into the carriage and off they went. The pastor and his wife stood for some time in the cold, waving until they could no longer see their disappearing son.

The trip was arduous, especially since it was wintertime, and the weather was not friendly, at all. The carriage was equipped with a closed-in cabin, with seats facing forwards and backwards, but no device for heating. Hans chose to face forward, but he knew that there could be changes to that, depending on who else was going the same direction he was going. His route would take him through Hamburg, Braunschweig and Magdeburg, before he would arrive at the university. He might have to stay in an inn here or there, as he made the necessary connections to Wittenberg.

As he was jostled on the rough road, he tried to peek out of the window, but it was totally frosted over, so that proved impossible. He was left with his thoughts.

*How will my relationship with Leah go, while I am at university? It will be a difficult few years, that is certain. Will my love for her cool during that time? Will hers cool for me? What about her thoughts of converting to Lutheranism; will she follow through on that? What if she doesn't? Would I want her then as my wife? Could we work together as a team, if we each have our own religion? What if we have children? How will they be raised?* Hans's thoughts were tangled, but every thought seemed to be a question, and there did not seem to be any answers. Everything pointed to a rather long time of separation, and there would be no opportunities for contacts with her, or with other young women, for that matter, until he was finished his studies. Well, at least Lutheran pastors could be married; the Catholic priests couldn't even do that. That was some consolation in his quickly forming loneliness.

• • •

"Well, have you decided whether you want to be a children's worker or a teacher, yet?" asked John Hildebrand at the supper table.

Heidi swallowed her mouthful of soup quickly and wiped her mouth with her apron, before replying. "I've been thinking quite a bit about it, and I wondered whether I shouldn't go into a convent and work with sick people," she replied with a very straight face.

"Now that is a radical change of plans," exploded Lizzy. "I thought you were converting so you could marry, so a convent wouldn't come into question."

"Well, it's going to be a long time before Jacob and I can get married, so I might as well spend that time in the convent, if I can't convert anyway." Heidi continued her charade mercilessly.

By this time Lizzy was all in a fluster, and rubbed her hands harder and harder together. She looked at John, who looked at her as though he thought she must be going crazy.

"I was only joking," said Heidi, with a smirk on her face.

"Oh you child," muttered Lizzy, smarting from the way she had been taken in by her daughter, aided and abetted by her father. "I must admit that I've wondered whether perhaps God is telling us all to go to a convent or a monastery, what with all the waiting we have before us."

"I have actually given my future quite a bit of thought, and I think I would enjoy being a schoolteacher, even though there are very few women who do that. Perhaps, if I stayed in a village such as Bad Oldesloe, I could enjoy it more, than if I went to a large city like Hamburg or Lübeck," said Heidi, now serious, so that even her mother could see that she meant what she said. "Where would I go to get the training I need?"

"I actually asked Father Daniel that the other day, when I met him in town," responded John. "He knew of some convents that actually offer Latin school classes to women," he continued, with a twinkle in his eye. "I also met Pastor Schmidt, and he mentioned that there was a Latin school in Lübeck that took Lutheran women. He didn't know whether they took Catholics. Menno doesn't know of any place that might be suitable, but he thought probably the Lutheran school would be more in touch with what we believe than the convents would be. Teachers in villages normally only have a Latin school education. Many only take a year, before they offer themselves to a village to teach. Most villages don't even have schools, especially for girls. Our Baron is very progressive, so we have a primary school here, for both boys and girls. Even the Mennist children come to that for a few years."

"What would I have to do to take Latin school in Lübeck?" queried Heidi. Her twisted lips showed her distaste for the idea.

"We would have to arrange for you to stay with someone in the city, and then you could attend classes at the school. It is too far for you to travel from here. That takes a whole day each way by horse," said John. "Do we know anyone in Lübeck with whom Heidi could stay, while she attends school there?" He looked at Lizzy for a response.

"One of the ladies mentioned in the store the other day that she had a sister in Lübeck. Perhaps she would have a place where you could board. I'll ask my friend next time I see her; she comes regularly to the store at the same time as I usually do." Mother's eyes brightened at the prospect that her daughter might be able to live with someone who had connections to Bad Oldesloe.

Heidi wasn't sure whether she wanted to leave home to go to school, but Hans had just left, so it seemed to be what people her age did. She guessed that she would soon adjust to life away from home and parents; in fact, the more she thought about it, the better she liked the idea. *What sort of feeling is it to have freedom to do what you want, without someone looking over your shoulder, telling you what to do and not do.* Yes, she would like to go to Latin school.

• • •

"Why do the weeks have to go by so slowly," moaned Leah. "I have only had one letter from Hans since he left, and that just told me that he had arrived and started classes. Nothing about where he's living, nothing about what he's doing with his spare time, nothing."

"Now, dear, he's probably very busy getting started with his studies and has no time to write letters. Or, like most students I've heard about, he has no money for postage," suggested Eva to her distressed daughter.

"I know, I guess, but still, it is hard to be away from him for such a long time. Working in the store helps to keep the sadness away during the days, but in the evenings, I miss him terribly."

"What are you doing about learning what it should mean to become a Lutheran?" Mother changed the subject, hoping this would brighten up her daughter's spirits.

"Nothing, I guess. What should I be doing? Pastor Schmidt didn't give me anything to do, to prepare for baptism or membership."

"You will have to learn to read German better, just like Jacob is doing. He's reading his new German Bible to help him with that, and he has gotten some other things from Menno, to give him practice."

Mother's suggestions were not hitting the right nerves with Leah. She was not interested in books and reading. She needed practical things to keep her occupied. Marriage and a family would provide that. For the moment, she was simply bored, because she had nothing useful to do, except to help around the house and look after her younger siblings. "I want to talk to Hans. That would help me more with my German than anything else. I don't want to spend my time reading books, even if they would help me with the language," she wailed. "Girls don't have to read. They don't have to know everything that's going on in the world. I've heard that someone thinks the world is a round ball. Everyone can see that it's flat, so why should we believe that kind of story? Just because someone read it in a book or newspaper doesn't make it true."

"I often wish I could read better," said Mother, "I think we need to know as much as possible about our world and about what we believe, because raising children makes us mothers have to answer lots of questions. Would you be interested in working in a class Menno is starting for children, to teach them the basics of Bible stories? You would be working with Tina Dyck, who is in charge, but you would help control children who aren't listening carefully. This will be held every Sunday before church service."

"Would Menno accept me? I suspect he knows that I plan to convert to Lutheranism. Would I even be a good person to have with the children of Mennists, learning the Mennist teachings?" Leah was not quite sure where she stood in relation to others within the Mennist church.

"I'm sure it would be alright with Menno. No one said that the person who would be helping needed to be baptized at all, or a church member. They just need someone who could help control all the unruly boys in the group, so that the experienced woman can teach them the stories," Mother replied.

"It would be good for me to help out with the children, I think, so do I need to see someone about volunteering for the job?

Mother was somewhat surprised by her daughter's sudden willingness, but she recovered without showing any telltale signs. "You could stop in at the Menno Cottage on your way home from work and talk to Menno himself about it."

• • •

Menno was producing another book. He could be found at the Menno Cottage almost night and day. His health was deteriorating, but he was more concerned about his wife's and his son's health. They seemed to have come down with something severe. Both had extremely high fevers, but the local person among the Mennists who had any medical knowledge couldn't determine what it was. It seemed to be out of the ordinary, perhaps one of the terrible sicknesses that gripped the area from time to time. Still, Menno needed to finish this book. His people needed this instruction. He better go home, though, because he had already stayed several hours, and there was no one to look after Gertrude and his son. Wearily, he packed up and put his coat and cap on, and began walking home, his cane landing hard for each step, and his gait halting and painful, as he made his way down the road to Wuestenfelde.

All was quiet as he approached his house. There were no lights burning. He entered, took off his coat and cap. He lit a candle from the fireplace coals that were still glowing and proceeded to the bedroom that he and his wife shared. She lay perfectly still under the covers. As he approached the bed, he realized that she was no longer breathing. She had passed on to meet her Creator. He brushed his hand across the cold cheeks and turned away. Slowly he made his way to the other room, where his son lay. He, too, had gone to meet his Maker while he was gone.

With torn heart, Menno sat down at the kitchen table, cupped his face in his hands and began to pray. "Lord, you have given and you have taken away. Blessed be your Name. I thank you, that you gave me a family, and that they knew you, before you claimed them back. I still have two daughters, so I am glad. Blessed be your Name."

After a short time of grieving, he thought it best to inform Jacob Derksen about the deaths in his family. There would have to be funeral arrangements, and it was still winter. Slowly he put on his coat and cap again, gathered his cane, and proceeded to the Derksens' house.

"I have come to give you terrible news," he greeted Jacob at the door. "Gertrude and David have just gone to meet their Savior. The fever took them while I was at the print shop."

Jacob put his arm around Menno and brought him into their family room. Eva, when she heard what had happened, got out some cider for the men and poured a couple of cups for them. Jacob led his guest to the table and showed Menno a chair, into which he painfully plunked himself.

"Is there anything we can do for you? Is your other son near here?" Jacob was almost at a loss to know what could be said to his spiritual advisor, who was himself now suffering terribly.

"We will need to make funeral arrangements, and one of the women will have to prepare the bodies for burial. Would you check with Jake, whether there are some coffins available for us to buy? Jonathan is still in Holland, and I don't know how we can contact him. He continues to move about, to avoid detection." Menno seemed to have everything under control, as he usually did.

"I can go and prepare the bodies for burial," said Eva, who had helped with this tender task on several occasions.

"I will ask Jake whether they have any coffins in stock at the shop. If not, he can build them in a couple of days," stated Jacob. "You must be dreadfully upset right now. Have you had anything to eat? Eva, could you heat up some of the stew we had leftover, and get Menno something to eat, please? I will contact the other deacons, and we will plan for a funeral in three days." It was Jacob's turn to have everything under control.

As Menno ate, and Jacob and Eva drank cider, there was a deep silence in the room. At this time, Jake and Leah both entered the room. They had come from different directions, but had come home at the same time.

"Gertrude and David have passed away of the fever," said Eva quietly. The two young people went over and put their hand on Menno's shoulder, giving him a slight squeeze. They both loved him deeply and respected him and his family very much. His grief touched both their hearts.

"Do you have any coffins in the shop, Jake," asked his Father gently. "We will have to have a funeral in a few days, and we need two right now."

"Why yes, we built some in just the past few days, so we have some ready. I could go right now and get them, if I could get a horse and wagon," Jake replied.

"That can wait until tomorrow, and you can get a wagon from the Baron's livery stable then," said his Father.

Jake nodded his agreement. "Who is preparing the bodies for burial?" asked Leah.

"I will do that myself, unless you wish to help me," suggested Eva.

"I would count it an honor to help you do that," replied Leah, wondering what she was letting herself in for, but convinced that it was the right thing to do. Her mother nodded her approval and her commiseration in her daughter's bewilderment and apprehension.

Would you like to sleep at our house tonight?" Father asked Menno.

Oh, I hadn't thought of that, but thank you anyway. I think I will go back to the Cottage and work a bit longer, and then sleep there. I have a mattress there, and some covers," Menno replied, showing the strain of his loss and yet, of his desire to finish the book.

• • •

Baron Bartholomew von Ahlefeld was full of plans. He could hardly concentrate on eating or sleeping, much less anything else that went on about the manor or the estate. It was a good thing he had men like Abe Voth and John Hildebrand around to supervise the crews. Other areas seemed to be working well, too. The town council seemed to function well, keeping things going on an even keel, as did the councils in the villages surrounding Bad Oldesloe, so he could devote his time to his plans for the future.

*We'll put the hog barn right there, where the wind won't bring the smell over the manor all the time, like it does now. We can put the livestock barn near it, over on this side, so that we can share some of the equipment needed in both barns. We'll need a ramp to the loft of the livestock barn, to keep hay and beets for winter feeding, and we'll need a large room with bins for the pig feed. The waste pile can be between the barns, to make for the shortest distance to transport it, and it can be gotten away from there quite easily for spreading on the fields.* His mind raced, as he sketched and doodled on one piece of paper after another. *How big should I make the barns,* he wondered, *I think I could increase my capacity by another time, and still be able to market the hogs and the milk. The young cattle could be put into a large open enclosure at one end, and the milk cows and little calves at the other end. Do I want to include the horses? No, I'll leave them in the present livery stable. We can rebuild that once we're done with all the other building. Now, what about fences where I can keep specific cattle separate from others, when needed? They can be built over here, on that side of the barn, with a door, maybe that should be two doors, leading into these enclosures.* On and on his mind raced, as his vision for the estate developed into something he could aim at in his building plans.

*The barns will be made of brick, and bricks are not easily to be had in his area. Perhaps I should develop the clay pit on the side of the field near the pond. That might make the whole project a bit easier. Where will I get the men for this? If I send 50 of them to Vienna, I won't have enough to make bricks and build at the same time. Perhaps I'll have to first make the bricks – that will take some time, for they have to be fired properly, and I'll have to have a furnace built for that, before I can even start on the other. We'll also need a place where we prepare the clay for the molds. Oh yes, and where will we store the bricks once they are made? This project is growing bigger than I had anticipated. Do I even have the money to begin such a venture?*

Careful calculation of what the various parts of the project would require led him to the conclusion that he could manage the finances, provided nothing went wrong in the meantime. At this point his attention began to be drawn toward the actual plans for the two barns, and his quill was kept busy sketching ideas for the various parts of each barn, which he then added to a master plan for each of the buildings. Soon he had what he considered a working plan for each barn. Each would involve time-saving design, proper ventilation, and plenty of room for the animals to develop normally. At length he sat back in his chair and viewed both the plans for the barns with some satisfaction. He was glad that his eye was clear and his vision for buildings was acute. *I will show the plans to Jacob tomorrow. Oh, wait a minute, I must first plan the brick kiln.* Off his mind went in another flurry of creative activity.

*Let's see now, there is a small drop in the land right here, and if I put the clay mixer here, I can use the drop to fill the molds, which would then be taken here for firing. When they are finished being fired, they will have to stay over here to cool, before we can store them over here. How many men* will I need to do each part? We will need about ten to dig the clay out of the ground, plus two drivers, to put it in wagons to haul to the mixing site where we'll need another five to mix the clay and prepare it for the molds. A chute should suffice to transport the wet clay to the molding area, where we'll need four to channel it to the molds and prepare them for firing. The furnace will have to be tended – I'll need a lot of wood, too, which will require three or four for cutting and hauling – and the kiln, too. Those will require two men each, no wait, four for the kiln, as they'll have to move the heavy molds full of clay into the furnace. Then, it will take another four to take them out and clear the molds and get them ready to fill again. Storage – yes, I'll need five men with wheelbarrows to take the bricks to where we'll stack them for storage, but that can't happen until they are cooled. Oh, yes, we can simply dump them into this lower area to cool – another chute will take care of that – and then take them to the storage area, which should be down on the same level. From there we can get them by wagon as we need them.

Having now completed the details of the planning to his satisfaction, Bartholomew retired to his private room, where his butler prepared him for a sound sleep.

# Chapter Thirteen

Spring made its way slowly into the area. Some days were warm, and brought out feelings of gardening and planting; other days were blustery and cold. For a week at a time, it would rain steadily, and then remain cloudy for days thereafter. Finally, the middle of May had come, when it was considered that the final frost had come, and planting of gardens and fields could start. The weather continued variable, but spring flowers had been evident in abundance for about a month already. Snowdrops had come in March, poking their cheerful heads up through patches of snow and ice clinging to the soil in sunny areas.

Wuestenfelde was not rejoicing in the new life that permeated every breath of air. There was a pall of darkness and gloom over the area, as another of the frequent epidemics that decimated populations raged through the village. The few that were strong enough sought to meet the needs of those too sick to care for themselves. No one understood the principles of transmission of such diseases, so precautions only included cleaning of utensils and cloths used in bathing patients in their homes. There was no trained doctor among the Mennists to measure out medicine or take temperatures, and the refugees were loath to call on the Catholic doctor in Bad Oldesloe. Experienced Mennist women, who had been through a previous time of this occasional visitation, were in high demand to help with those who were the sickest.

The fever raged for two days, and then came the turning point. If a person's resistance was too low, the temperature increased, and the person died on the third day, and if resistance was high enough, there was a turn for the better. No one knew what made a person more or less resistant than the other one, so it seemed like a roulette game, as to who would live and who would not.

Eva would have been one of those who could have helped, but she, too, had succumbed to the fever, as had Isaac and Schaetzli. The other family members seemed to be resistant to the sickness, so they were called on to care for the less fortunate. The same pattern occurred in every home throughout the village. Bad Oldesloe had even more sick people than the village. Even the Baron's estate was not exempt; his workers were as decimated as were all the other families in the area. Children seemed to be less resistant than adults.

Anxiously the Derksen family watched, as Eva and the two children lay in their beds with high fevers. The house was small, so there was no way to isolate the sick from the well. Foreheads were bathed in cold water to ease the temperature, but little else was known that would help to alleviate the fever or other symptoms accompanying the sickness.

Special prayer meetings were called by the Mennist deacons, to bring their people's needs before a high and holy God, seeking for mercy for the helpless victims lying in house after house. At first they and Menno had visited the homes in the area, giving encouragement wherever possible, and soliciting the help of those who were able, to assist in homes where there was no one to care for the sick. The bells of the Catholic church tolled in the morning, the afternoon and even the evening, as procession after procession made its way to the cemetery. The Lutherans, too, used their bells to announce another funeral. Spirits were subdued and morose, as family after family said farewell to loved ones and friends.

Leah moved between her mother's bed and the children, seeking to comfort them with a cold cloth on the forehead and making them drink a bit of water each time. She looked anxiously at Father, who stared lamely into the distance, unable to fathom the sorrow that might come upon his household, and immobilized by fear that he could lose precious loved ones to the rampaging fever. Jake was busier than ever at the shop, preparing coffins for the inevitable burials that must take place. His colleagues were reduced to a minimum, as one after another of the workers fell ill, too.

As the third day dawned, everyone became tense, waiting to see what the signs might be of recovery or demise. Jacob and Leah kept their vigil, continuing to cool their patients, and watching for any telltale changes in the symptoms. All the while, they hoped that they would not be in the second wave of those who succumbed to the fever. Perhaps their ignorance of medicine was a blessing; it kept them from theorizing too much, and kept them close to their patients, who needed their presence more than anything.

The day dragged on, grey and foreboding, as the weather had been since the sickness first made its presence felt. Clouds continued to block the sunlight that might have brightened the spirits, and depression settled over village and town. Those who cared for the sick were now so tired that their actions were mechanical and thoughtless. No one had gotten a full night's sleep since the plague hit. Tempers were short, and children were restless and ill cared for. No one had time to give them, unless they happened to be those who had become feverish.

Aron and Frederic were no exception. They were not sick, but those who normally cared for them were desperately sick, or were caring for their sick loved ones. They became more and more unmanageable, and Jacob's patience was worn thin by constant vigil. Almost brutally he got them into their jackets and boots and sent them to play outside, where they would not be such a nuisance to the sick inside the house.

The hours wore on, and Leah found herself dozing on her chair, catching her eyelids falling and then awakening with a start. Jacob was dozing in his comfortable chair, exhausted from the days and nights of vigil behind him, and relieved that the noise of the young boys was now in the distance outside the house.

Leah woke from one of her lapses, and found her mother sitting up in bed, drinking water from a cup by her bedside. Hurriedly, Leah got up and tried to make her mother comfortable. She then departed into the other room, where Isaac and Schaetzli were lying. To her horror, both had succumbed to the illness and lay still in their beds. Slowly, mechanically, she moved back to the room where her mother and father were. They could see on her face that something dreadful had taken place in the other room.

"They are with Jesus," she spoke softly. "He has taken them to become His angels."

There was deep and tremendous grief, but the bodies and spirits were so worn out, that it didn't show on the parents. Eva laid her head back on the pillow and drifted off to sleep, while Jacob stared blindly into the fire burning on the hearth.

"I will go tell Menno," volunteered Leah, "and then we'll have to get them ready. Oh, I wish we could inform Jake, so that he could get us a small coffin and a larger one." Her elders gave no response, but she slipped out the door. On the way, she informed the two boys that they were not to go into the house until she came back, which of course, made them all the more curious about what was going on inside. They promised not to go in and continued with their play.

• • •

Heidi was not active. She was lying in bed with the fever. Lizzy bathed her forehead with cold water, as she watched her daughter lose the will to fight back against the disease. She had just returned from classes in Lübeck for a short spring break, but had become sick during the night. John had heard from various others, that nearly every home in Bad Oldesloe was affected by the fever. For two days and nights the vigil continued, as it was continuing in the other homes around, with hope hanging on a change for the better in the patients. Heidi's body continued to burn with frightful heat, and her mother sponged off the perspiration with a cool wet cloth, trusting for the fever to break on the third day, as they had been told it might.

The grey sky announced the beginning of the third day, as it had to the Derksens and to every other family in the area. Nothing in the externals could bring up the flagging hopes of either those who were sick or of those who were caring for them. Their spirits continued also to be grey and hopeless, as they went about the necessities of caring for themselves or their loved ones.

"Where is my mathematics homework?" moaned Heidi, then, "Is that you, Jake?" Her fever had elevated to the point where she was delirious, and one subconscious thought ran into another. Her mother wiped her forehead with the damp cloth again, and her daughter drifted back into a fitful sleep, tossing from side to side in the bed.

"I'm hungry," the clear voice woke Lizzy with a jerk. What had she just heard? Was she dreaming? She looked at her daughter from her chair by the bedside, and was amazed to find that she was no longer in the bed beside her, but was brushing her hair by the mirror over her dresser. "I'm hungry," she repeated.

"Oh, my dear, I'm so glad you're better," exclaimed Lizzy, hugging her daughter and sobbing her relief. "I'll fix you something as quickly as I can. We've hardly eaten, either, since you got sick, so I think we need to celebrate with something special. Let's see, what can I fix?" her words trailed off, as she left the room to go to the kitchen.

"I will fix a bath and get cleaned up from all this sweat," Heidi showed her resolve to get back to normal life.

• • •

What a change in the Schmidt household from just a few days before. Hans had been able to find a ride with a coach bound in their direction, and was to be home for a week. The first day had been especially nice, as the sun shone brightly and the family was able to share some precious moments together around the evening meal. That night, however, Hans developed a high fever, and for the next days, it raged higher and higher. Mrs. Schmidt did what she could, and Pastor Schmidt called the doctor, who came on his way around to practically every house in Bad Oldesloe. He also did not know any better way to lower the fever than to sponge the forehead with cool water, and to give the patient as much cool water as he could drink, and as often as he would drink. He told them that the fever usually broke in three days, or got worse. Everyone knew what getting worse might mean, and eyes dropped. The grey pall of depression settled over the Schmidt household, as it had on the houses around. Pastor Schmidt kept being called out to perform funerals for the victims, so he was unable to look after his own loved one. He soon discovered that Father Daniel and Menno were having the same problems in their parishes. Then he heard that Father Daniel had also become ill, and the priest from the next parish had to bury both his own dead and those of Bad Oldesloe.

Hans's fever raged day and night, and his mother's loving hands cooled his forehead with cool cloths. Between times, she dozed in her chair beside the bed of her son. The third night was the worst, as the temperature rose even higher, and delirium set in at various times. In the morning, Mrs. Schmidt gazed at her son intently, hoping to see some glimmer of hope in his condition, but there seemed to be none. He lay quite still and colorless, breathing heavily and erratically. Suddenly, she noticed a stirring in his eyelids, and a rasping sound from his mouth, as he tried to speak. With great effort, he opened his eyes and looked at her, seemed to smile, and tried to say something. It was all lost, however, as his breath left him, and he slumped back onto his pillow.

With a shriek, Mrs. Schmidt covered her face with her apron, then bent over her lifeless son and sobbed uncontrollably. Her husband found her that way, when he arrived back at the house an hour later.

Baron von Ahlefeld was agitated, as usual, but not for the usual reasons. Normally, he was agitated, because he had something planned, and he was anxious to get the plans into action. This time, it was the opposite. He had plans, but they were not getting put into action. The fever had hit many of his workers' families, and he was having difficulty just looking after the everyday things that needed to be done in his barns and shops. His plans for building new barns were on hold for the time being, until this epidemic had run its course. These pesky epidemics, he thought, they come around somewhere in the area from time to time. No one can predict them, and no one knows what to do about them, when they do come. The doctors are helpless, and so are the priests. What good is religion, when it can't even help a headache and fever? How long would it take, before he could get through the spring seeding in his fields, and the other work on the estate, and then be able to begin construction of his hog barn? He was anxious to get going on this project, which had been absorbing his thoughts all winter, and which he deemed to be more important than anything else that should happen, including an epidemic.

He thought of calling his steward, but then he remembered that his manager was also affected by the fever, and was unable to answer his call. How was he going to get started, if he couldn't even find anyone from among his own workers, who was fit enough to handle the project? Duke Adolf had sent a messenger yesterday, informing him that twenty of the fifty men he had sent to Vienna had also succumbed to the fever, and were lying at death's door. *Cursed plagues! Why do they have to come, when you least expect them, and when you want to do something important, like building bigger barns or defending your country against the Turks?* At least to this point, there didn't seem to be anyone in his immediate family that had gotten the fever. *I guess we're just stronger than everyone else,* he mused. *You have to be strong to get by all the things that life throws at you these days,* he continued in his self-glorification. *The Emperor has*

*claimed back The Netherlands and Flanders, and his henchmen are perse-*
*cuting both Lutherans and Mennists everywhere, and now we have the fever*
*here. Bah! Where is God when you need Him most?*

• • •

The fever left as quickly as it had descended on the area. The tattered remains of families supported each other in their grief, and spring work was begun. Although the natural energy that comes with increasing sunshine and longer days was not as evident in the depressed people, things must be done, so those who were able got back to work, and those who were unable stayed home to recover their health and strength as they could. Every traditional remedy known to anyone was tried.

Seeding was due, but first the plowing and harrowing needed to be done, to prepare the soil. Then every available person, male or female, was conscripted to help out in the fields, in order to get the crop in. Private fields and gardens needed to be planted, and fruit bushes and trees pruned for best crops. The blossoms brought color back into the surging landscape, and people's spirits began to pick up a little.

The Baron spoke to Jacob about starting on the construction of his barns, and once again, he offered him the larger house on his estate, from which he could work more efficiently. Jacob said that he would bring his family over on the following Saturday, so they could get settled in before work on Monday. His concern about leaving John with the hogs, just at the time when the litters were demanding the most time was allayed by the Baron, who said that a young fellow from one of the families that had recently joined them from the Netherlands would join John in the hog barn. Every available worker would be put to work on the construction project.

Leah was heartbroken, as was to be expected. Having lost both her younger siblings and her boyfriend had taken a terrible toll on her emotions. She went to work in the store, but smiled at no one. She did her work robotically, without passion or thought. At home, she was a brown study every evening, as she helped around the house. Eva had not regained her strength quickly, so Leah was left to do most of the heavy cleaning and washing in the evenings.

Jake had been especially busy making coffins, as the store had run out quickly. The shop had a way of doing them simply and hurriedly, when necessary, and those where the only kinds that were used to bury most of the dead from the fever. Only Hans was buried in a coffin that had carved features and fine wood, with bronze handles.

Heidi bounced back to her normal self fairly quickly, and went back to Lübeck to continue her education in the Latin school there. After all that had happened during her time in Bad Oldesloe, she wondered whether anything could ever get back to normal. She and Jake had not been able to spend any time together at all. In fact, they had only waved at each other in passing one day.

The move was accomplished with the use of a wagon and team of horses from the Baron's livery stable. Eva and Leah had packed everything as well as possible, though they lacked any boxes or crates to put things in. Everything was piled helter-skelter into the wagon, and off they went to the new house, where they spent some time trying to figure out where their things should go. They were pleasantly surprised to find that the Baron had left quite a bit of furniture in the house, to which they could add their own, and after some juggling, they found that they could be quite comfortable in their new home. After a good night's sleep, they were refreshed and joined their friends in the Mennist church in Wuestenfelde the next morning. It seemed strange walking the opposite direction than before, but after some light remarks about this, everyone thought it was quite nice, especially since the sun was shining, and there seemed a promise of good weather to come. The brilliant flower beds added a cheery note to their conversations, and brightened their spirits considerably. Menno's message reflected on the hope that believers have in the Lord. When He comes again to take his own home, we will not have to endure suffering anymore. It had helped him, he said, in honor of his wife and son, who had died earlier in winter, to plant a tree the previous week in their honor. People could see the Linden tree near the Menno Cottage, and this would remind them of the blessed hope in Christ. This seemed to be a message for everyone's heart, and all went home cheered by his words. On the way to their new home, Jacob and Eva talked about planting three trees to commemorate their three children, Henry, and the two that died in the fever epidemic. That seemed to provide a bit of emotional release to their broken spirits.

Thus spring rolled by into summer, and the work connected with the fields and gardens took on greater energy again, as one crop after another was ready for harvesting, and hay needed to be cut for the next winter. Jacob could not do anything on their private plot, so Jake needed to do this after his work in the carpentry shop. Eva, Leah and the small children had to see to the garden work.

Leah enjoyed working with the children in the village on Sunday mornings. She found satisfaction in seeing each one learning biblical truths and repeating memory verses, and she was adept at helping them with their handwork, that Tina Dyck provided to reinforce the lesson of the week, and to keep mischievous hands busy. There were fewer children than there had been in early spring, but the children that came seemed to appreciate the time they had together before the adult service began. That, they knew, was going to be torture beyond anything they could ever imagine – having to sit absolutely still for a whole hour on a backless bench, while their parents sang the old hymns and listened to a sonorous message by Menno or one of the deacons, who took services in Menno's absence. Many a child could vividly remember – almost feel – the pain of what had happened recently, when they had not behaved according to expectations. Mennist fathers executed swift and painful justice, when nervous young bodies caused disturbances in church. The side door to the building was used often for such hasty exits, and the sounds coming from outside after this departure were not conducive to quiet spiritual meditations for the older ones. Aron and Frederic were some who remembered well what happened when they misbehaved in church, so they found quiet things to occupy their thoughts, and knew every nail in the building, having studied them in detail through many a long service.

As time went on, Leah began looking over to the other side of the building, where the men and boys sat, whenever she could sneak a peek that way without causing her mother's concern to be raised. There were several young men her age there that she had never really noticed before. They seemed very intensely interested in what was being said, and no one seemed to notice her attentions.

At the end of one service near the end of May, Menno announced that the following Sunday, everyone should bring some extra food along, and the whole congregation would have a church picnic together by the Baron's woods nearby. With that, the service was dismissed, and the buzz of excitement mounted, as people left the building to go home. *What should we bring,* thought Leah. *What should I wear? Do I even have something suitable for a church picnic? Will anyone even notice me?* Her thoughts played with these thoughts all the way to their home on the Baron's estate.

# Chapter Fourteen

Sunday morning dawned beautifully, with a rosy glow in the eastern sky forecasting a lovely day ahead. As the wagons gathered near the church, and as crowds of people flocked into the service, Leah hoped she stood out in her new dress that she had sewn during the week. She had borrowed a dress from Heidi that she liked, bought some cloth that was as bright as she thought she could get away with, and began to stitch a lovely dress for herself. She also got a new undershirt to complement the outer garment, so that she felt very fresh and feminine. It had been hard losing Hans, but she had seen some things through this trial that she had never seen before, and she had grown up greatly through it all. She was pleased to see that several of the other young women had also sewn themselves new dresses, so that the gathering began to take on the aura of a spring parade of all the lovelies in the congregation. Eva sat looking straight ahead, obviously trying to keep her eyes from her daughter and the other maidens, for she did not approve of such attention-seeking dresses. To her, it seemed that this was the top of a very slippery slope, leading to certain destruction at the bottom, but she realized that the whims of youth, even her own daughter's, must be patiently tolerated, so she held her peace. Needless to say, the young men's gaze did tend to wander over to the other side of the congregation, where there was much to attract their attention.

The service was actually quite interesting, emphasizing God's handiwork in creation and in man as its crowning achievement, with God's love and power in creating new life in the repentant sinner as application. When they were dismissed, the group left for their wagons or carried their baskets on foot, as they made their way to the edge of the woods, where an inviting meadow awaited them. Along the edge, small oak and beech trees formed a low wall of rough and smooth trunks, capped by brilliant green spring leaves. Behind them, mature trees loomed against the sunshine, which played in fanlike rays through the leaves, resulting in spots of light on the forest floor, while the rest of the area was bathed in a blanket of shadow from the canopy above.

Deacons instructed the families to bring their food dishes to a central place, where a long table had been arranged on saw horses, so that each could sample the others' wares. Eva and Leah brought their baked fava bean dish and their sorrel leaf salad. At the dessert end, they placed a platter of Leah's tasty bread Kringel, with a plate of butter and a bowl of honey beside it, and a knife for spreading. There were other examples of fine cooking, for the Mennist women were known for their resourcefulness in this, and occasional baked goods, for few had an oven, as Eva had. Spreading blankets over the grass, which had been mowed for the occasion, the congregation found places where it could eat.

As the last dishes were placed on the table, Jacob asked that all should bow their heads in silence, and he offered a simple prayer of thanks for this wonderful spread. After that, he invited the oldest ones to come and begin to dish themselves up from the table, while the children tried to get a glimpse of what to them seemed like very quickly disappearing bounty. Finally it was their turn, and with help from parents and older siblings, the young ones were also dished up, not always to their liking, with the nourishing meal before them.

Mothers with small children tended to sit near each other, to help keep an eye on their offspring, while the men went to another area to discuss things of interest to them. Older children formed a gang that roamed noisily through the ranks, until their fathers brought a rough order by insisting that they join their mothers and younger siblings on the blankets. Young people were left to fend for themselves, and that they did with alacrity, both at the table and with each other. Seldom did the young people have an opportunity to get together as a group – there was no young people's group for them. They were expected to work as adults, and any social contact must come at other times, such as this picnic. With time-honored activities, the groups of young men and young women drew closer and closer together.

Leah was keenly aware that she was the center of interest to several of the young men. She, at least, felt that she was the most beautiful of the maidens present. Her new floral dress was very attractive, and she had tied her auburn curls with a matching ribbon. She was dimly aware that the other young women felt the same way about themselves and their clothing, but that didn't matter. She felt good about herself, and that was all that mattered to her. Across the group, speaking with some other girls her age, she noticed the long blond hair that looked very much like Heidi's. Yes, it was Heidi. She had joined them for the picnic. Leah waved to her and smiled warmly.

It was not until then that Leah realized that something strange had happened to her during the past several months. Not only had she lost Hans, but she was feeling more comfortable with the Mennist women and girls. Now, she was also finding herself feeling more comfortable with the Mennist men and boys. Had her desire to convert to Lutheranism been only something that related to Hans? Heidi didn't seem to have lost her desire to convert to Mennism, and had used this open-air picnic as a means to spend time with Jake. Leah wasn't sure, but for now, it was great to be young, attractive and outside in God's wonderful world, looking at a relatively good choice of young men that might be available for her to pick from. God had taken Hans away from her; she must find her way to a new life without him, and find someone she would!

As they moved through the line for dishing up food, Leah became aware that a certain young man was quite close to her. She turned and smiled at him, and made a comment about one of the dishes on the table that looked especially interesting to her. The man blushed and remarked that it was what his mother had brought, and he, too, thought it was very good. Together they took some onto their trenchers and selected other items that appealed to them. The young man introduced himself as Heinrich, and said that he had recently moved to Bad Oldesloe from Friesland, where his family faced open persecution for their faith. They had heard about the Baron's protection for Mennists, and had found their way surreptitiously to the estate. The Baron had given them a house that had recently been vacated in Wuestenfelde, because the previous people had moved to a house on his estate.

"That would be our old house," Leah remarked, "My father was asked to head up the building of the new barns for the Baron, as he has had bricklaying experience, so we were offered a bigger house on the estate."

"Then I'll be working for your father," said Heinrich, noting to himself that it might be a good idea to get to know this woman's father very well. "By the way, my family name is Gerbrandt, so, I'm Heinrich Gerbrandt. I have never worked with bricks, but I'm willing to learn, and your father can probably teach very well. I notice that he is one of the deacons of the Mennist church here," he continued the banter with Leah until another young man, who had hovered nearby, butted in.

"I'm Jonathan Wiebe, and I will be working with your father, too," he offered. With that, two other fellows, who had sauntered up to the table, also volunteered, "I'm Fred Fast, and I'm working in the fields with the four-ox teams," and "Hello, my name is Helmut Froese, and I will be doing the accounting for the Baron's new projects."

"Let's see now, said Leah coyly, I'll begin with the last one first and try to remember your names. You are Helmut, you are Fred, you are

Jonathan – and let me remember – you must be Heinrich. I won't try to remember all your last names right now. I am glad to meet each of you. My name is Leah Derksen, and I am now the oldest child in our family. My brother was executed for his faith last winter, and two of my younger siblings died of the fever. Jake, over there, is my brother. He works in the Baron's carpentry shop. He took the job that Henry had before he left us. I had a boyfriend, Hans, who also died of the fever." Why had she said that last bit? It wasn't any of their business, although she knew that at least three of the fellows knew of her previous interest in Hans.

Leah spent a delightful afternoon visiting with the young men who had introduced themselves to her, as well as with the other eligible young women and their interests. Quite a large group of young people were now part of the Mennist church. She was able to place some of the men whose younger siblings she cared for in the Sunday Bible lessons, so it was easier to recognize them by name and by face. She had not felt so free and talkative since before Henry had defaced the statue of Mary in the Catholic Church.

It was time to go home, so everyone pitched in and helped to clean up the things on the table. Each family claimed its own, and there were the usual arguments about this item or that, that looked similar to one at home, that was mistakenly taken by the wrong person. Finally, the table was taken down and the pieces put into a large wagon with a matched team of dark brown Belgian geldings pulling it. Their blaze flashed wide, as they turned their head from side to side, and their white fetlocks were well trimmed. The harness was burnished and well-oiled, and the wagon showed the crest of the Baron, who had donated it for use today. Walking in groups, or riding in wagons, the crowd walked back to the village, and some, like the Derksens, continued on to the western outskirts of Bad Oldesloe, where Altfresenburg Manor was located. Walking by the Menno Cottage, they noticed a fresh young Linden sapling, planted there by Menno a couple of weeks before. They were reminded that they would plant some trees to commemorate their children, but they decided that these should be fruit trees, each bearing its own fruit, as their children would have done, had they lived to realize their full potential. Henry's would be an apple, Isaac's a plum, and Schaetzli's a cherry tree. Jacob agreed to find saplings of those kinds to plant. The Baron had an orchard that included several varieties of each of those fruits, so it should not be too difficult to find a suitable sapling for each.

• • •

Pastor Schmidt and Mrs. Schmidt were devastated by the loss of their youngest son. Hans had been their special love in their late middle years, and now he was gone. He had shown such promise in wanting to follow his father into the ministry. Now there would not be anyone to follow in father's footsteps. The older sons all had their own careers, and their daughters were married to successful businessmen. None lived near them in Bad Oldesloe. All had their own families, so there were grandchildren, but they were far away in Lübeck or Hamburg. Should they consider moving to one of the large cities, to be near their children and grandchildren? If so, which children? Which grandchildren? Then, too, they had spent almost all their married life in this town, and their congregation had grown to love them. What were they going to do?

"I have been talking with Eva Derksen lately, sharing with them in their loss, too, and I see a strength in those Mennist women that I don't find in our church," ventured Mrs. Schmidt.

"Yes, there is something that is deeper than just the teachings they follow; there seems to be a different life within them, that pulls them through such difficult circumstances," replied Pastor Schmidt to his dear wife. "Still, I don't see anything very different between what they believe and what we believe, only the severity with which discipline is meted out in the church on those that don't live up to expectations. For many in our church, it seems that they aren't sure what they believe about cardinal Christian doctrines, but they have been baptized and they faithfully attend church. The rest of life doesn't seem to have been affected by their declaration of faith." The pastor rambled on, revealing that he, too, had been giving some thought to the differences he saw between the Mennists and the Lutherans. He was well aware that there were few distinguishing characteristics between the Lutherans and their Catholic fellows. To many it seemed more important that they were Germans, and that their prince either believed as the Pope did, or not, and that made a difference in their pocketbooks.

"I've wondered whether we should convert to the Mennists," reflected Mrs. Schmidt.

"I wondered, too, but I have decided that our congregation needs us more," said Pastor Schmidt, more decisively. "We simply need to read in the Scriptures more, now that we have the Bible in German, and find our solace in God Himself. If I preach a more evangelistic message, perhaps they will respond with a bit more godliness in their lives," he continued. "It is, after all, the Holy Spirit's work to convert souls, not the Church's. We are called to be faithful, not to be Christ, Himself. Besides, the Duke's order must still be obeyed, even though there hasn't been anything more said about it. No one may convert from one church to another in his realm, and that includes the Baron's estate. Perhaps, however, it would be permissible for us to attend the Mennists picnic, which I heard they are having this afternoon."

Mrs. Schmidt agreed that this seemed the better option for them. They would faithfully maintain their work in the church God had placed them in, and trust Him for the results in people's lives, but would be more open to the Mennists and learn from them what spiritual life was really all about.

When they returned from the picnic, where they had visited with Jacob and Eva Derksen and Menno, Pastor Schmidt reached for his new Bible and found the first chapter of Matthew, and clearing his throat gently, he began to read the genealogy of Jesus to his dear wife, noting especially that Jesus' birth was narrated in simple, clear language, but noted that prophesy from the Old Testament had been fulfilled in his birth. He also noted that Joseph, who was somewhat of an outsider to the marvellous things that were happening around him, was obedient to that which God revealed to him. Already comfort was settling in, just knowing that God's Word would minister to their need. They would continue to read a chapter each evening and see what God would teach them.

• • •

Heidi wondered at the fact that she had been spared, when so many had not survived the fever. *What is that supposed to mean for me? Am I something special to God, that He had taken special notice of me in my affliction? Am I supposed to do something for Him in return? Since Jake did not get feverish, is he a superhuman, to be feared, revered, or worse yet, both? Then there is Eva, who also recovered. How am I like Eva? Not much,* Heidi thought. Then again, she had no idea what Eva had been like when she was her age. Perhaps she, too, had been impetuous and frivolous at one time. *Does age do that to people? Do we really change that much, to make us the kind of harsh disciplinarian that Eva seems to be? She really isn't that harsh,* rationalized Heidi, *she just looks that way. Will I begin to look that harsh, as I got older? Every generation went through different circumstances as they matured, and that reflected itself in the faces of people as they got older,* she decided. *My circumstances were different, and I will look different. At least, I hope so.*

The time for her next class had come, and Heidi slipped into the seat that had become familiar to her over the past months. It was fulfilling to study. One learned so many things from the teachers, who knew their material well. Some lacked instructional skills, but their knowledge of their subject matter was superb. Heidi couldn't understand it, that some of her classmates compared the teachers on the basis of how well they taught, rather than on how valuable was the material that they taught. She enjoyed digging into the books to find out for herself what it was that she should learn. Her reverie was cut short by this teacher's monotonous voice beginning the lesson of the day. *How can a person take such interesting material and spout it out in such an uninteresting way? Oooops!* She caught herself criticizing the teacher in exactly the same way she was criticizing her colleagues for criticizing their teachers.

Class ended, and Heidi had hardly heard any of what the teacher had droned to the class. She left for her room, which her mother had arranged for her with the relative of her friend. This arrangement had worked out well for Heidi, for it gave her privacy, but also kept her in touch with friends of the family. The house was not far from the Latin school, so Heidi could easily walk to and from classes. Olga, the woman of the house, was a good cook, so the meals were excellent. She kept a clean house, so Heidi's room was always spotless. North German hospitality lacked nothing, when one had a doting grandmother looking after one's needs.

Religion class was most interesting. Of course, it was the Lutheran religion that was being taught, and that often conflicted with the Catholic upbringing that Heidi had experienced. She no longer crossed herself when prayer was offered, and she had long since stopped repeating the rosary, but there were times when her background did not want to step quietly out of the way to make room for something new. A religion based on tradition carries with it many things that remain in the subconscious, even when one doesn't believe the doctrine behind it any more. She found herself curtsying and looking for the water in which to dip her fingers when she entered the school chapel for the daily service, held by a Lutheran pastor connected to the school, as she had been taught to do when she entered the Catholic church in Bad Oldesloe, where Henry had destroyed the image of Mary. What about Mary? Her mind began to wander again during the message. *There is no image of Mary in this chapel, but there is a crucifix with the body of Christ on it, as there is in my church. Is it Mary herself the Mennists don't believe in, or is it just her image? I'm not so sure just now.* The pastor droned on and on, so that Heidi began to doze. As the service closed, she was awakened to hear him say, "May the grace of our Lord and Saviour, Jesus

Christ, the love of the Father, and the fellowship of the Holy Spirit rest and abide with you, Amen."

Grace, love, fellowship – those were the important things to believe in. Those were the things that went with a person from one service to the next. With those, spiritual life was meaningful. The religion teacher had said, that Luther had come to his conclusions, when he realized that "the just shall live by his faith." *Faith ties it all together, then,* she reasoned. *God gives his grace and love freely through Christ, and the Holy Spirit brings about fellowship, all through faith.* In the glow of this epiphany, Heidi walked home to her house, went to her room, and prayed that God would reveal Himself to her, as she exercised her humble faith in Christ, and that He would use her in whatever way He might see fit. Having done so, she made her way to the table, where Olga had the evening meal waiting for her. As they ate, Heidi began to tell her about what she had learned that day. Olga, being a devout believer herself, could only smile her agreement, as this young Christian began to testify to what God had taught her.

Heidi, however, was not satisfied with the amount she understood about this truth. She must find a Bible and read for herself the deeper truths connected with faith, grace, love and fellowship. She asked Olga whether she had a Bible in the house, to which the older woman answered no. She knew that Luther had translated it into German, and perhaps there was one in the school. Heidi considered it for a moment, trying to think of whom she could ask at school. *Perhaps the small library attached to the front office might have one; I will ask the school secretary tomorrow. Or, perhaps the pastor who spoke in the chapel service would know. He teaches religion classes at the school, so he might even use a Bible there. Maybe a Bible can be bought for very little, after all, Jake had one – oh yes, that one had been a gift from the Baron, so money was no object.* For the moment, she must content herself with reminiscing about what she had heard in chapel and what she knew from her childhood in the Catholic church. She went to her room and finished her homework for the next day and prepared for bed.

• • •

Baron von Ahlefeld was perplexed. This wasn't the first time in his life he had experienced this condition, but this time, he was really perplexed. Now that the fever had run its course, those who had died were buried, and life was returning somewhat to normal on the estate. He had taken his wife and family on a wagon ride on Sunday afternoon, and had seen the large gathering of Mennists near the woods, enjoying a spring picnic in the warm sunshine. In spite of their suffering and their losses, they were celebrating the newness of life that was pulsing through all of nature.

Grass was green, trees were in blossom, rows were beginning to be seen in garden plots. Everywhere there was vibrant life, and these people were sharing in that life. The deaths of the past weeks had been put behind, and they were enjoying the fact that they had been spared to appreciate this outburst of God's gift of life once again.

As the groom guided the matched team of black Belgians along the country roads, the sound of the harness and the crunching of the large steel-rimmed wooden wheels on hard soil was accented by the smell of the horses and the harness, and together, they made the Baron's family more aware of the spring scenery they were passing through. White and red blossoms alternated with fresh green leaves, as each tree pushed hard to reach the warmer sunshine. Soon the fruit would begin to show in miniature green form, and begin the summer's process of maturing and ripening. The promise of good-tasting fresh fruit was already tempting the children. As they rounded one last bend before coming back to their yard, they passed the barn under construction. One wall appeared to be finished to its intended height, and others were at various stages of completion. Soon it would be time to hoist the heavy timbers for the roof structure and seal the building from the elements. Jacob and his crew were doing good work; the Baron seemed quite satisfied with his project. And amid this excitement, they reached the door of their mansion and got out of the wagon, leaving the groom to put the horses and wagon away.

The thoughts of seeing the Mennists celebrating in the open kept coming back to Baron von Ahlefeld all evening. *How can they celebrate after losing so much?* Perhaps he should be looking into what they believed, in order to find out where their inner strength lay. That strength might be able to be found for himself and his family, even without joining their radical group. Perhaps he should read in the Bible himself, and his thoughts trailed off . . .

# Chapter Fifteen

The sunny, cheerful days of the past weeks turned to long weeks of dreariness and depression. Rain and cool weather hampered crops from sprouting well, and that which came got drowned in puddles on the fields. It became obvious to everyone that the wheat crop would not be sufficient to sustain all the people on the estate. Added to that, the Duke kept up his pressure on the Baron to rid himself of the Anabaptists, and to disallow any conversions. At the same time, he demanded more soldiers to replace those who had died in the fever epidemic. A new religious menace had come their way, namely the Calvinists. Already in Switzerland, France, Flanders and southern Netherlands, they had taken root among the leading people. Whether their attraction to this new sect was the result of their desire to get away from the clutches of Rome, or to experience the exhilaration of knowing that they were saved, we will never know, but there was definitely the desire to get away from the tax burden that the Catholic Church laid on everyone, and the works-based salvation preached by the Catholics did not provide assurance of salvation.

Emperor Charles V had become even harsher in his efforts to save his empire from the encroachments of these religious sects that drained away the revenues from his and the Pope's coffers, and wrought havoc among the Catholic faithful. The whole system of empire had been based on the supremacy and indivisibility of the Catholic Church. It was from this concept that Charles himself maintained his power, as he had allied himself with the Pope to enforce Catholic faithfulness in the Holy Roman Empire, which he as a Habsburg ruled. He received this powerful position almost as a divine right from God Himself, he thought. This empire extended from Hungary and Poland westward and southward across Europe to Spain. Germany's three hundred petty kingdoms belonged to him. By marriage contracts of past rulers, Charles, the grandson of Ferdinand and Isabella, was a Habsburg, and thus a claimant to the throne of the empire. Charles was a devout Catholic, inclined by his zeal to enforce Catholic doctrines on everyone in his realm, and he was doing so with vigor.

The Americas, recently discovered, were being given the gospel along with the stealing of their land and resources, notably gold, to enhance the glory and purses of Spain. Slave trade had begun against the principles of the Pope, as European epidemics had wiped out large numbers of the natives in both Central and South America, and the sugar plantations that Charles had introduced needed workers. Spanish galleons carried sugar to Europe, tools and utensils to Africa and the Americas, and slaves from Africa to the Americas, making a profit in all three directions. Spain was in its heyday the most powerful nation Europe had ever seen, and Charles wanted to keep it that way. He knew, also, that religion played a large part in keeping a nation strong and rich, and the Catholic religion was designed to enhance this plan.

The Catholic Church, however, had misjudged the impact that the simple monk from Wittenberg would have on its holdings, both spiritual and temporal. Luther was not alone in his dissatisfaction with Mother Church. Scores of others were preaching reform from within the Church, and not a few were willing to go much further and separate from the Church to go according to their own beliefs. The ones that concerned Charles were the ones that used the Bible as the basis for their separatism, and those were the Lutherans, the Mennists, and the Calvinists. Each Protestant division took its stand on a different point of doctrine, but all had in common the belief that the Roman Church had pushed its control too far, and that it was not living up to the biblical standards it purported to teach. All were agreed that tradition was not sufficient basis on which to build a church; the Bible needed to be that foundation. Therefore, Charles had used the Spanish Inquisition, which quickly turned from its original targets of Muslims and Jews, to the Protestant sects that were springing up all over northern Europe. The Lutherans and Calvinists, in turn, used similar tactics to persecute the Anabaptists, now mostly congregated among the Mennists, for they, too, believed in the universality of the church or Kingdom of Christ. That is, they believed that all those who lived in any given principality should have the same religion, be it Catholic or Protestant. Therefore, the Mennists were as much of a nuisance to the Lutherans' and the Calvinists' concept as they were to the Catholics,' for they refused to participate in any government, believing rather in the separation of Church and State. Mennists, therefore, were now being persecuted from three religious sides.

Now that Charles had abdicated in favor of his son, Philip II, and had become a guest in a monastery in Spain, it fell to the new monarch to tighten the net around the pesky Mennists. Hence, the continued pressure from the Duke, who was Lutheran, to not allow conversions to Mennism. In Friesland, where Menno had begun his ministry, the Anabaptists were now beginning to be called Mennonites, and this name began spreading, as more and more were forced to flee their homeland and seek safety elsewhere. The Estate was growing continuously, as family after family, or bedraggled individuals who had lost all their loved ones, found refuge in its borders. The bad weather might have played a role in keeping those who were hunting them from finding the hunted ones.

The Baron did his best to provide for the newcomers, but was taxed to the limit in finding suitable housing for everyone. Some had to simply move in with existing subjects. Since the Derksens had a larger house than others, this was asked of them, and they responded with characteristic charity. His projects, notably the barns, required a lot of extra workers, and these seemed to come out of the very soil itself, as one after another came to offer his services, in order to keep his family safe and intact.

Jacob was thankful for the extra help, and he worked feverishly to keep all his hands occupied. Scaffolding had to be built, taken down, moved, and rebuilt a number of times, for the building was large. Bricks needed to be hauled from storage to the building site, stacked for immediate use, and transported to those who were laying them. Mortar needed to be mixed, put in hods and lifted to the men on the scaffolds, who were laying the bricks. Tools had to be repaired and sharpened; the blacksmith shop was busier than it had ever been. Wheelbarrows and hods needed to be where they were most needed. Extra horses had been bought in neighboring areas to make the transport possible. Jacob was busy each day with the planning and running of the job. The Baron kept coming whenever he had time, to see how progress was being made on the barns. He had gone to building both barns at the same time, partly because he had enough workers, and partly because he wanted to see the project completed. His dream was being fulfilled before his very eyes.

Abe Voth's carpentry shop was extended to the limit to prepare the beams and rafters for the barns. The sheer size of the buildings was more than they had ever had occasion to build, so equipment and shop size were not sufficient to accommodate the necessary work. Men who had some experience working with wood were sent to the shop to help, and that added to the need for more space. An extension to the present building was built of wood, and new tools were acquired, to make it possible to handle the massive beams that would be required, once the brick walls were completed. The brick walls had already been notched to receive the beams, which were being prepared in the shop by Jake and the ever larger crew. These beams were so large that it required most of the men present just to move them for that preparation work. Oak is heavy, and the Baron was not sparing any expense in getting the best wood for his barn. Oak is also very hard and difficult to carve with ordinary tools, so the process of cutting mortise and tenon joints was slow and arduous. Because it was not common to use nails or screws to hold the joint in place, but rather, a simple oak pin, a hole to accommodate the pin must be bored through mortise and tenon to anchor the joint later. This necessitated careful measuring and fitting, for it was not possible to change the hole once the beams were in place above the brick walls. Some joints were made with oak wedges holding the beams in place, and these wedges had to be made to order for each joint. This work, in addition to that of repairing wagons, wheelbarrows and brick hods, kept the crew busy day after day.

The field workers had it hardest. The soggy ground was impossible to work; it stuck to every implement and refused to turn over. Horses and equipment became mired in the muck. Those who worked with oxen found it a bit better, as oxen seemed to find better footing in the wet, slippery mud. There was a sense of hopelessness, however, for nothing seemed to want to germinate and grow in the cold, wet soil. Time after time they prepared the ground as best they could and reseeded it, but the weeks went by, and hardly any evidence could be seen of results for their labor. It was now too late for the wheat to mature in time for harvest. Bartholomew von Ahlefeld, being the far-thinking and progressive thinker he was, began to wonder what other types of grain could be brought in that would take root in this weather and provide for his ever-increasing populace. He began to ask those in his noble circles whether they had heard of any plants that might be of help. Horticulturists over all of northern Europe had been working for years in seeking to improve the plants that were used as staples; surely there must be something that would provide winter sustenance for his people.

Barley was the grain that showed the most promise, for it had the shortest growing season and would normally germinate in cool weather. The Baron ordered seed and had it delivered to the estate, where his field workers had already prepared the soil one last time. The weather looked promising, and off they went to broadcast the seeds across the harrowed fields. Within three days, little green shoots could be seen popping up all over, except where puddles still covered the fields. Most of these had been drained, to get as much soil prepared as possible, but some had nowhere to drain into, so they remained to punctuate the even flow of the green in the fields. Barley was not as fine as wheat or rye, but it was nourishing, and it could possibly be ready before the first frosts came.

Bartholomew von Ahlefeld was relieved to see the new growth that might result in a crop. It was almost as though his prayers were being answered, for he felt very keenly his responsibility for his subjects. Indeed, he counted it as almost a religious duty to protect them and provide for them. Besides, his barns would be ready before the crop came, and would provide storage for the grain, once it was harvested. The brick construction would prevent rodents from taking it away or spoiling it. Yes, he could rest a bit easier now, having done what he could to make sure there would be enough in the granaries to feed his people.

One thing, though, made him wince occasionally, and that was one of those problems that seemingly only got worse by thinking about it. He seemed to be getting people fleeing to the estate who were different from the Mennists he had received before. Some were similar, he reckoned, but others didn't seem to be Mennists at all. That DeFehr family seemed to come from a completely different religion than the Dycks, for instance. What the difference was, he did not know, but he would have to keep his ears open, to see whether having them would disrupt what was happening on the estate. He knew one thing; he would enforce his edict of non-conversion on all of them. What they came with, they could keep, but they could not change and remain with him.

• • •

Eva Derksen was stretched to the limit, looking after her family and the DeFehrs, who had come to live with them. They were a Calvinist family who had experienced similar persecution as they had earlier in their flight from the authorities, but in Flanders, before they had left for Holland. From there they had come to Fresenburg Estate, having heard of it through Mennonites in Holland. Their way had also been difficult, and they had lost one child to the fever, too, before they had arrived on the estate. They still had four children, but the mother was exhausted from the extended time of hiding by day and traveling by night that had brought the family to the Baron's estate. Eva, in addition to her own remaining children, had the four, plus Annemiek, the mother, to care for. The DeFehr children were all as young or younger than her youngest, including a baby a few weeks old, so her hands were more than full with the extra work.

As she cared for Annemiek, the women talked about the faith that had brought them to the estate. Eva had never heard of Calvinists, so she was doubly curious what her new housemate believed.

"What brought you to the estate?" she asked, as she brought a bowl of soup to the woman in her bed. She continued to fuss with the bedding and with a pitcher of water and a cup beside the bed, while she lifted the youngest DeFehr onto her lap, so the little boy could see his mother.

"The magistrates had put a price on our head, and we had to leave. Ben was very active in spreading our faith, so he was targeted especially by the authorities, both in Flanders and then in Holland. He is working with Jacob now, because he had some experience in bricklaying, too, as we moved from place to place, but he is a preacher at heart," replied Annemiek, with a bit more animation in her face than she had shown before.

"Are you also Protestants then?" asked Eva innocently.

"Oh, yes, John Calvin insisted that salvation was only by the grace of God, who is sovereign over every person and determines who should be saved and who should not be saved," Annemiek was now becoming the preacher that she claimed her husband to be.

"Doesn't a person have to choose to be saved?" asked Eva, wondering about the idea of God's sovereignty.

"Why yes, but God predestines some to choose and others not to choose to believe in Christ for salvation." Annemiek's concise description of Calvinism seemed to confuse Eva even more.

"But you must be baptized as a believer, not as a baby, to signify your faith," Eva was changing the subject, she thought.

"No, no, no. We baptize babies, because we believe they are part of the Kingdom of God, and that He will predestine them to become true believers, because we dedicate them to Him at birth," Annemiek's theology had definitely reached well beyond Eva's comprehension. She changed the subject, this time to a non-religious topic.

"This rain is going to ruin the crops, and we will be hard-pressed to have enough to eat next winter."

"Perhaps, but God is sovereign, and He will look after His own, as He has since our turning to Him," countered Annemiek. "Ben says that this is just to test us, to see if we really do trust in God's ability and desire to provide for His people, His called and predestined ones. We could choose right now to live entirely rebellious lives, and God would still love us and save us, because He predestined us to be His children."

Eva suddenly found a reason to retreat to the kitchen with a tribe of tiny feet following her, and a baby in her arms. She busied herself with finding suitable food for them all and seeing to it that they were satisfied. She then led the tribe to the bedroom that housed their mattresses on the floor, as well as the bench-beds they had for their own children, and she put them down for a nap. It was raining steadily outside, so it was not practical to shoo them out of the house.

Having a bit of time for herself now, she sat down, reached for her crocheting, and began hooking quickly and efficiently. Meanwhile, her mind kept going over the seed thought that Annemiek had planted, that God predestined some to salvation and others to damnation. That was harsh. Menno never taught anything like that. In fact, he emphasized that salvation was contingent on their maintaining their faith. Annemiek said it wasn't. Which was right? She would ask Jacob tonight, for she did not have the answer to that question.

• • •

Pastor Schmidt and Mrs. Schmidt were also faced with the problem of the Calvinists. The DeFehrs had approached them about attending their church, but asked that they also be able to share what they believed with their church congregation. Their thought seemed to be, that Lutherans would convert to Calvinism, if they only knew what the doctrines were. The Schmidts had listened patiently to Ben and Annemiek's description of their beliefs, but had not agreed on what was involved in predestination. They agreed that God is sovereign, and that He wants all to be saved, but they did not believe that God predestines some to salvation and some to ultimate damnation. In their view, a person, or a family, chose to become part of God's family. There was a secular kingdom and a spiritual kingdom, and some things were part of the secular and others, of the spiritual kingdom. All people moved in both kingdoms, depending on what part of their lives they were considering. In this way, the Lutherans distinguished between secular authorities and spiritual authorities. Thus, the Schmidts and the DeFehrs parted without the agreement that would allow the new family to share their faith among the Lutherans. That isolated the DeFehrs in the estate community, for they could not find fellowship with any of the other three religions. They would try to reach the Mennonites, and the Derksens were a logical first step. Perhaps they could also talk to Menno himself, but he was traveling so much that this seemed almost impossible.

The Schmidts, meanwhile, were faced with the need to further study their faith, which had already been shaken by the death of their youngest son, who looked to be the one who would further the cause of the Lutheran Church Reformation.

• • •

John Hildebrand had a new problem. The worker who had joined him in the hog barn when Jacob was moved to the barn building project was another Mennist, but he had died in the fever epidemic, and now the new man assigned to him seemed to be a Mennist with different views of what it meant to be one. He claimed that the others on the estate were Frisians and he was a Flemish Mennonite. John had not heard that there was a difference among the Mennists, and the term Mennonite was totally new to him. Because of his unique situation in regard to the enforcement of non-conversion on him and his family, he now had a new situation to evaluate. His name was Abraham Dyck, which he said was a name originating in Flanders, where the Flemish brand of Mennonites had originated. His family had emigrated to Holland some time earlier, and now, he claimed, many Mennonites in Holland had adopted the Flemish brand of Mennism. The Friesians were individual-based, having been independent farmers all their lives, while the Flemings were industrialists and merchants, having grown up in large cities like Ghent, Brugge and Antwerp, and thus had grown up dependent on each other. Therefore, he said, they tolerated individual differences more, and were less critical about the outward signs of being a Mennonite, such as dress, than the Friesians were. He claimed also, that this brand was more tolerant than the Friesian brand was, when it came to involvement in the community, too. Mennonites in Friesland, where Menno had begun his teaching ministry, were now somewhat equally divided between the two factions, Abraham claimed. From what little John had seen of the Dycks, as compared with the Derksens, they were less tolerant of each other, when it came to church government, than the Friesians he had come to know. They seemed to like having very strong men at the helm, where Menno and the others seemed to allow more freedom of expression in their church. John would have to ask Jacob Derksen what that all meant, when he met him next.

• • •

Leah and Heidi became closer friends in their frustrated search for a faith that would sustain them. Heidi had not given up her struggle to find a true belief in Christ that was biblically based, and she asked pointed questions in her classes, while Leah's struggle between Mennism and Lutheranism continued unabated. Heidi had obtained a Bible from the school temporarily, and had then been given one by a kind staff member, who thought thereby to help her resolve her search for the Truth. She read feverishly in the New Testament, taking special note of the teachings of the Sermon on the Mount, which seemed to her to reflect the teachings of Menno precisely. Leah, not one to read avidly, contented herself with the practical experience that her job at the store and at the children's ministry gave her. She, too, asked pointed questions whenever possible, to further her knowledge of what the Bible taught, and what the various churches believed about these things.

Heidi's long letters to Leah reflected her journey of faith, while Leah's tortured notes reflected hers. As Heidi expressed what she was learning through reading in her new Bible, she awakened a desire in Leah to also find out for herself what God taught. She asked Jake whether she could read in his Bible in the evenings while she was at home. It was not easy for her to grapple with the long German words, and the old Gothic script nearly turned her eyes inside out, but bit by bit, she struggled along.

At times, she had to ask Jake for help with the meanings of unfamiliar German words, and that improved her ability to understand the language as she went along. Together, she and Jake decided it would be a good idea to look up texts that Menno or the other preachers used in their messages, in order to figure out the context in which they were found. This proved quite interesting and profitable, for they began to see where the ideas expressed in the messages originated. Jake was too busy in the shop to do more than this, but he was deeply thankful to his sister for opening up to him, so that they could share their questions with each other. Both were growing in their spiritual knowledge by doing so together.

One subject that came up was prayer. *What is the purpose of prayer? Is it really necessary? Does it actually help to pray? Does God hear prayer and answer? Are there conditions involved in having prayers answered?* As they studied the New Testament together, and as Leah corresponded with Heidi, the answers for each of them began to come out of the Word itself. As they learned more and more about the efficacy of prayer for the Christian, they were moved to begin to pray for the harvest, which seemed very uncertain. They also prayed for the families who had lost loved ones to the fever and for the families that had joined them on the estate recently, especially the DeFehrs.

Another topic that interested them was that of assurance of salvation. The Calvinists seemed totally assured of their personal salvation, but neither the Lutherans nor the Mennonites seemed to be able to rest assured that they were part of Christ's family, even though they had followed the teachings of their respective leaders. The Catholics for certain did not know whether or not they were saved. Most expected to spend many aeons in purgatory, before being purified enough to be allowed into heaven. The Lutherans, as far as the young people could determine, believed they had the way to God figured out, but were never quite sure that their salvation held them in that theological grip. By this time confirmation, which had been a part of Catholic tradition, was also supposed to confirm a Lutheran's faith to them, but there seemed always to be a question whether the young person being confirmed was really a believer, or not. No outward change of life seemed to occur in their declaration of faith. Jake began to correspond with Heidi about that question, partly because he felt he should be showing her some affection while she was absent. As Leah and Jake continued to study the Bible together, this seemed to be a prerequisite for true salvation. Then they were exercised whether there had truly been a change of life for them, or whether they had become the products of a different tradition. Thus, their thinking was stimulated daily by what the Bible was revealing to them, and as they discussed these thoughts with each other and corresponded with Heidi about their questions.

*How am I ever going to figure out what it all means?* questioned Leah to herself. *Every church seems to have its own interpretation about the things in the New Testament, and we have to make up our minds about things without even knowing enough to make a good decision. I guess I'll just have to stick with the practical things I've learned and not worry about the new things I hear about every day. Someone at the store said the other day, that we now have a different kind of follower of Menno among us, and Mother was saying that the DeFehr family that stays with us is called something like Calvinist, whatever that means.*

*Why does love have to be so complicated,* Jake thought, as he tried to express his thoughts to Heidi in his letters. *Does Heidi go through all these questionings in her mind, too? Are they even connected, or am I just connecting them in my own mind?*

*Is it always the same, when a person thinks about what to believe?* thought Heidi, as she wrestled with the teaching she was receiving at the Latin school, and comparing it with what she read in the Bible. *The Lutherans obviously have very strong beliefs, which they claim come from the Bible, but when it comes to putting them into practice, I don't think they do as good a job as the Mennists do. Mennists may be quite old-fashioned in how they express their beliefs in regards to dress and lifestyle, but they certainly live up to what they say they believe, much better than the Lutherans. I wonder what Jake thinks about the rules set by the church.*

The only one who seemed to remain on the outside for the time being was Jacob Derksen, who was so busy with the barns, that he had no time to consider theological issues. The rains had made his work doubly difficult, but he had devised ways of protecting his workers from the worst of the downpours, and he had kept the crew busy throughout the long wet spring, to the point where the project was ready for the second stage, namely, putting up the roof trusses.

# Chapter Sixteen

Summer came late, but it finally came, and when it came, it came with a heat that seemed unbearable. Bad Oldesloe is in northern Germany, where heat is not the major factor defining summer, so even what was in actuality a moderately hot summer, seemed to everyone to be exceedingly hot. The heavy rains of late spring had provided ample water to make the hay fields produce an abundant first cutting, and the verdant grass sprang immediately to action in starting on a good second cutting. The livestock, at least, would thrive over the next winter.

Some vegetables produced abundantly, others hardly anything at all. Eva and the other women worked daily in the gardens, nurturing every plant with motherly care, to ensure that everything that would produce anything at all, would produce as big a crop as possible. Peas, for instance, produced constantly, requiring almost daily picking, shelling, and drying. Drying was the only way that such legumes could be preserved for the long winter months. Pole beans did not do well, but fava beans did better, though not abundantly. These, too, were carefully removed from the pod when they were dead ripe, and then dried for winter use. Beets and turnips produced fairly well, but the soggy soil around them almost turned to concrete as it was baked by the summer sun. The women worked very hard to break up the hard earth near the plants, to provide oxygen and moisture to the roots. Potatoes, the new crop introduced by the Baron, were almost a total loss, as the soggy soil and cool temperatures of late spring had caused the leaves to grow out of proportion to normal, and delayed the flowering. The hope of all was on the barley crop, which, if somewhat normal, would sustain them adequately, if not in luxury, through the next winter.

Friesian Mennonites had always been an agricultural people, and those on Fresenburg Estate continued in that tradition. Some had worked in various trades, and sought to find work in those occupations. Those who joined them later from Friesland were mostly cloth weavers and merchants, as they had originated in Flanders, and they soon found ways to produce and sell cloth, first in the community, and then in markets farther afield, always keeping in mind to stay within the bounds of Baron von Ahlefeld's protection. Having made contact, however, with cloth merchants in the Hanseatic cities of Lübeck and Hamburg, they were able to market their wares throughout the Baltic Sea region. Their superior knowledge of spinning and weaving, learned in the most fashionable markets of Europe, stood them in good stead now, as they were forced to start afresh. They were joined later by Flemish Calvinists, who had also been involved in the cloth industry in Flanders. From a business standpoint, this was good, as they had the latest spinning and weaving techniques in hand, while the Mennonites had learned second-hand from refugees to Holland.

Ben DeFehr had been a cloth merchant, and he soon left the work of the hog barn, where the smell was repulsive to him, and marketed the cloth woven by those who had come as spinners and weavers. Flax became a more important product on the estate, and the Baron saw to it that proper machinery was made available to process the flax into linen, so that the demand for his weavers' products could be met. Wool was still a staple for cloth, so sheep farming was also stepped up. Should the barn be converted to a lambing station, or left to house his dairy herd and horses, he wondered. No, he would simply construct an open shelter for them near the field where they would graze, and that would suit just fine. As soon as Jacob had finished the first stage of the barns, he was commissioned to build this shelter, which would only have three sides of bricks, with short walls coming in from each side wall, to shield ewes and lambs from the cold, wet North Sea wind, that seemed to blow all year, but was especially bad during lambing season.

Jacob then began to build houses for the new people that had come to the estate. He drew plans in the evening, seeking to design them as best he could, according to the plots of land available and the needs of the individual families. For the merchant and weaving families, there was no need for a barn, so he built city houses for them on lots in Bad Oldesloe, where they could obtain everything they needed at Janzen's store. They could purchase fresh vegetables from the farmers, and dried food in winter, as well. The Baron's butcher shop was constantly supplying meat to those who did not do their own butchering, and his bakery supplied a variety of breads and pastries. The dairy supplied fresh milk, cream, butter and cheese.

Now that the DeFehrs had their own house, the Derksens had more room for themselves, and Eva especially, enjoyed her increased freedom to care for her own family. She planted a huge garden, which she nursed as though she was trying to revive it from a sickness. Everything produced as much as was possible under the meteorological circumstances, so she was pleased that a good store was being laid up for the coming winter.

The Mennonite Church, for so it was now being called, due to the large influx of new folk from Friesland and Flanders, where this was the common name for followers of Menno Simons, was growing so quickly that the old building which was serving for worship was much too small. Whenever possible, services were held out of doors, to provide room for everyone. Menno, who was the Bishop, and Jacob and his fellow deacons were planning how they could build an adequate building for their worship. The Baron could see that this was becoming a necessity for the congregation, and he gave them his hearty approval.

Because it would be a very simple structure – the Mennonites did not believe in having ornaments and required no large altar area or choir loft, nor did they have instruments – it would be basically four brick walls with an ample thatched roof.

They would need to make bricks, for there were none left of what had been made the previous year, but they could use the moulds and the kiln that the Baron had made available for the barns earlier. A crew largely made up of men that had been on the project with Jacob began work on brick making immediately, in preparation for the beginning of construction. Timber was secured for the long rafter trusses that would be needed, and for making the benches and pulpit. The floor and platform would be made of flagstones laid into mortar to make a watertight surface. It would be acoustically very live, but it would help the voice of the preacher to carry better. A room beside the sanctuary could be used to have a special service for the children, so as to keep the noise down during the preaching. As the design took shape, Menno's and Jacob's hearts beat with anticipation to see the finished product.

• • •

Heidi's last examination was written, and she had passed all her subjects with good marks. In some, such as literature, rhetoric and writing, she had excelled. Mathematics had been a problem, but she had struggled through with enough understanding to make a passing grade. History and science were especially interesting, for their content exhilarated her. The new knowledge was fascinating, as information kept coming from explorations in the New World and from Asia, both of which had ships visiting them regularly. As the year had progressed, her desire to learn had increased to the point where she did very little else than study for one subject after another.

Now that the school year was finished, she made arrangements for her parents to pick her up. All her bags were packed when the coach arrived with John and Lizzy. They spent one night at Olga's, enjoying the gossip they shared that evening over a new drink that was made with crushed leaves from Ceylon – called tea – steeped in boiling water, before starting off for home together. Lizzy preferred hers without any additions and John preferred his sweetened. Arrangements had been made for Heidi to return to Olga's next fall, to complete her Latin school education, so that she could teach school in Bad Oldesloe.

Heidi's mind, always buzzing with this idea or that thought, was especially busy on the ride home. The jolting, bouncing carriage threw her into the wall and back into her mother's shoulders alternately, so she elected to sit cross-legged on the floor between the seats that faced each other front to back. Her parents smiled to see that their daughter hadn't changed in one respect. She was still the same active, tempestuous Heidi they knew, and their hearts warmed.

"Why does Menno teach that babies should not be baptized?" she began. Now her parents caught a glimpse of what was going on in her fertile mind. Without waiting for her parents to reply, she continued, "Martin Luther also believed that we are saved by faith alone, just like Menno teaches, but he baptized babies, just like Catholics do. I learned this in our religion classes at Latin school. I learned some other things that I wonder about, too. There are so many things that are nearly the same, but totally different, when it comes to what we believe and how we act on our beliefs." Her words seemed to come like gushing water that cannot be stopped, and as she talked, her actions became ever more animated, as only Heidi's could.

"In our classes with Menno, which we've been attending whenever he is in town, he has been emphasizing that a baby cannot exercise faith, because it simply hasn't got the maturity to be able to decide what to believe and what not to," began Lizzy, trying at times to remember exactly what Menno had said. "As a person grows, the mind is able to grasp things more clearly, until a person is able to decide what to believe, based on the evidence in God's word. The Catholic Church has always taught us that we cannot know what the scriptures mean, because we have not had their theological training, and only the church can interpret the Bible. Menno says that this is only based on tradition – the church has always taught it this way, so that must be the way it is. They say that they teach what the Bible says, but when we look for ourselves, we find that the Bible doesn't teach what the church has taught us. I believe Luther also found the same thing, and departed from the church over it."

"We've been duped by the priests long enough," broke in John. "I think we should go over to Menno's church now, secretly, and not wait on the Duke's orders not to convert."

"What happens to babies that die, or very young children, who haven't grown enough to be able to claim faith for themselves?" continued Heidi. She had been saving up questions for her parents, questions that had tormented her many a night, after she had been exposed to biblical passages and Lutheran teaching. Her Catholic upbringing had suffered a major blow day after day.

"We have to realize we are sinners, before we can be saved," said her mother matter-of-factly. "I guess God just keeps babies and young children for Himself until they can decide whether they have sinned or not."

"Some children do very bad things, even without realizing that, if this was done by an adult who knew, it would be a sin," countered Heidi.

"Yes, but the important thing is that a person must be old enough to realize his sin, before he or she can repent of it," John found himself digging quite deeply to come up with this bit of wisdom. Then he remembered, "Jesus said, 'They that are whole have no need of a physician, but they that are sick: I came not to call the righteous, but sinners to repentance.' I believe that comes from the Gospel of Mark somewhere."

"What is the difference between salvation and baptism anyway?" Heidi's questions seemed to penetrate farther and farther into her parents' hearts and minds, for they had been wrestling with the same questions.

"Menno says that baptism is only a sign of what has already happened in the heart of the person accepting this rite. A baby hasn't done anything or believed anything except that food comes from mother, so its baptism accomplishes nothing. The rite seems to be only something to remind the parents to train the child up in biblical truth, with the hope that it will someday confirm that faith that the parents have tried to give their child. One could equate it with circumcision in the Jewish faith. Every Jewish boy was circumcised the eighth day, to show that it was part of the Jewish nation, and to show that it subscribed to the Jewish faith. In reality, it was a sign that the parents would raise the little baby boy as a Jew. It accomplished nothing spiritually, says Paul in his epistles. As Christians, we are part of a spiritual Kingdom, not an earthly one; that is why we must enter it by faith." By now John was waxing quite eloquent. He had heard Menno well, and he had understood.

"How would you convert secretly? The priest would know immediately, and then the Bishop, and soon, the Pope." Heidi was skeptical, to say the least.

"I don't know," whined John, "but I'd certainly like to put that behind me. This going to mass every Sunday, and then sneaking to meetings with Menno is wearing your mother and me down."

"Maybe God has a surprise waiting for us," mused Lizzy cheerfully.

"I certainly hope so," said Heidi with emphasis. "Jake and I have been discussing the Bible in our letters, and we have learned many things from each other. God has many things He wants to give to those who believe in Him."

• • •

Jake went about his work in the carpentry shop with the precision he had always brought to whatever he did, but now with the precision that came from almost being a practiced journeyman. He had learned quickly under Abe Voth, and he had found numerous ways to test his skills, as the various projects on the estate demanded things from the shop, both big and small. He had learned what the properties of the various woods were, where each should be used and how it should be worked and finished for maximum strength or beauty. He loved wood, and working with it was a joy to him, as well as a soothing elixir for his mind.

As he worked on a beam for the new church, he began to think of what that church building might do for the community. He began to think of himself and Heidi, and how they might fit into the church together. *Together? How is that going to happen? Heidi is studying far away, and the Duke has placed a ban on conversions. Since Heidi's family are Catholics, they will have to convert and become Mennonites, if Heidi and I are ever to be married. What will that mean? Will they be safe on the estate, if they openly confess their faith? Will the Baron be able to protect them from the Bishop and his magistrates? There must be some way,* he thought. *Surely God hasn't brought us together in such a strange way, without wanting us to live life together as a married couple. Surely my brother hasn't given up his life for nothing at all.*

He continued to work on the beam, so he didn't notice Abe Voth coming up behind him. "Jake, I have something I want to talk with you about," said a voice immediately to his right shoulder.

Jake dropped his adze in surprise and whirled around to see who was talking with him. As he recognized Abe, he relaxed and smiled. "You gave me quite a fright," he laughed.

"I'm sorry, you were deep in thought, it seemed, as you were working, so I guess you didn't hear me coming," Abe apologized. "What I wanted to talk with you about was your future," began Abe carefully. "You have learned many things here in our shop, and you have become a very good worker. There are some things that I cannot teach you, though. We don't have the equipment that would be needed, and frankly, we don't need much of what is used in cities. Still, in order to be fully qualified as a master carpenter, you need more training and experience in special areas, particularly in making furniture, cabinet building and finishing work, maybe even wood carving. For this, you need to go to a shop in a large city, where beautiful things are manufactured and installed. I have looked into a shop in Lübeck that would be able to take you on in fall. Would you be willing to go there and spend the next year learning that part of the trade?"

Jake wasn't sure he knew what to think about such a move. *Will my parents be able to get along without me? Heidi is studying in Lübeck; that will place us together in the same large town. Will we be able to maintain our purity, if we are that close together without anyone to supervise us? She will be coming home any time now, so I could talk with her about that. Heidi is someone with whom you could talk about anything, so that doesn't threaten me at all.*

Abe waited patiently while Jake mulled over the various aspects of this proposal. Then, without further hesitation, he replied, "I believe that would be the best for me now, and I guess it would add another dimension to this shop when I return."

"I thought you would see this as the right thing," replied Abe. "I will contact the owner of the shop and make the arrangements."

Jake was not used to singing. This wasn't his particular gift. Somehow, however, a melody began to find its way into his mind, and soon he was humming through the percussive noises of the shop. Abe smiled and nodded, as did the other workers.

• • •

*That confounded Adolf,* thought Bartholomew, *he keeps reminding me not to let anyone on my estate convert. What does he think? The Peace of Augsburg in September a year and a half ago allowed every prince to choose the religion he wanted for his people. If the prince was Catholic, the people would be Catholic. If he was Protestant, the people would be Protestant. Can I help it, if there are three or four kinds of Protestants, and all of them come to my estate for protection? Why, Adolf himself is a Protestant. Why is he so insistent that no one should convert? Is he afraid of the Bishop? Hasn't he got a bigger and better army than the Bishop has? He's usually off helping his brother up in Denmark, anyway. Only if the Bishop comes tattling would he ever know that anyone converted anyway.*

The question of conversion had been coming before him regularly, as one Protestant group after another pressured him for permission to evangelize on the estate. There were still plenty of Catholics, and some Lutherans, but a growing number of Mennonites and Calvinists. Then, too, there seemed to be a new kind of Mennonite coming to the estate from Friesland and Flanders. They seemed to stick closer together and demand that everyone in their group act the same, or else they were cast out. The Friesians had not been quite that harsh in their discipline, though it was harsh enough, but they had been much more independent-minded about things. That had seemingly led to some quarrels among the leaders, all of whom thought God had given His whole vision to them, and them only. Now there was bickering among the Mennonite groups, as to which way was the right way. *I had better stay out of that one,* thought Bartholomew. *Then again,* he thought, *I probably couldn't stay out of it. The building of the new church will surely split the group in two, and then what? They would not think of sharing the building; the other group, whichever one it is, would be castigated as of the devil and banished from any fellowship with people in the other group. That seems unavoidable. I have let the Calvinists start their own services, and they brought someone in whom they thought of as their pastor. Since they are all involved in cloth production and marketing, they seem to stay together as a group and not cause too much trouble on the estate.* Above all, Bartholomew wanted a peaceful estate. He was not at heart a man of war, though he was an experienced military leader. Perhaps that is what attracted him so strongly to the Mennonites. They refused to go to war, even taking execution, instead of the sword.

*How can I solve this problem diplomatically, without causing too much disturbance among my people, and yet allow enough freedom for each group, to be able to practise their beliefs without fear? Being a leader of people is not an easy vocation,* he mused.

• • •

Menno worked feverishly at his cottage, writing and publishing one book or tract after another. His legs were not strong any more, but he continued to travel to places as far away as Prussia, where many of his followers had emigrated from Friesland and Flanders. The demand for more teaching was strong, as congregation after congregation looked to him for guidance in the doctrines that were to be taught, and in the way churches should be organized and led. What a believer could or could not do was always an issue. He wished that God would simply put a halter on a person when he believed, and lead him about like a horse, so that he wouldn't constantly have to intervene on points of disagreement on questions of what was worldly and what was not.

Now the Flemish way of belief had infiltrated the Friesian congregations, so that it seemed every church was splitting over whether it handled this problem of worldliness one way or another. His own co-worker and mentor, Dirk Philips, had become Flemish in his teachings. His brother, Obbe, who had ordained him to the ministry, had actually left the faith, it seemed, having become totally disillusioned by the fickleness of men. He seemed to have taken on himself the guilt of what his mentor, Jan Mattijs had instituted in Muenster. How could one so grounded in the faith suddenly turn and speak against it? Menno had no answer.

*Will our church hold together through the building program and after?* Menno wondered how God would intervene in this situation. Although he was of a very pacifistic mind, he could see that sincere people would drift to the stricter church discipline of the Flemish church. The individualism of the Friesians would have to give way to a more democratic church approach, which recognized the values of the group above those of the individual. Basic doctrines, such as salvation, baptism and the need for a Christian life were agreed upon. *It is those other thorny issues that will divide. They will probably continue to divide people long after I am gone,* Menno reasoned.

• • •

Leah enjoyed her work at Janzen's store, and she participated with satisfaction in the children's ministry at the Mennonite church. The physical situation of the latter was not conducive to having the children's attention, but she and Tina made the most of what they had. Tina proved quite resourceful in her teaching methods, thinking that happy and involved children learned better than sullen and still ones. Sometimes Leah came home worn out from all the things that Tina had the group doing, which she also did, to show solidarity with the head teacher.

Mr. Janzen had also added a section to the store, to accommodate the growing number of customers. He had also added some items that were now coming available in the great markets in Hanseatic cities, like Lübeck and Hamburg. One day, as Leah was stocking the expanded shelves during a lull in the shopping, she overheard the Baron's wife talking with one of the leading women of town. "You know, Bartholomew is wondering what to do about this strange business of people not being able to worship as they believe. The edict of the Duke seems silly, what with the Peace of Augsburg having given each prince the right to choose the religion of his region. Our Duke is Protestant, and we lean towards Protestantism, so what should be wrong with people converting to a Protestant religion, if they want?"

As the women came into the store, they ceased their conversation, but Leah had heard enough to satisfy her that those in authority were trying to make a way for people like herself to convert, if they wished. And there were the Hildebrands, who, like she, had postponed their baptism indefinitely because of the decree. She had caught her breath at the bit of gossip that she had overheard, realizing that there might be the opportunity soon for her to become Lutheran. She thought of what it would mean to her – more freedom to live as she wanted, to dress as she wanted, and to be friends with whom she wanted. She would soon be a part of the majority in the estate, and possibly in all of northern Germany.

Then, her involvement with the children's ministry came to mind. Tina told the Bible stories simply and clearly, with great animation and practical application. Leah had become very familiar with the teachings of Jesus during her winter of helping with the children. She began to wonder whether her desires for freedom from the constraints of Menno's teachings were really an improvement over the beliefs that her family had. Her mother was severe, to be sure. Her hair was always pulled back into a bun, which she pinned rigidly into place, and her clothes were always plain and single colored – usually black, grey or dark blue. Over her long dress, she usually wore an apron that covered most of the front of her body, so that her femininity was undetectable. Then again, she was fifty and couldn't be expected to dress like a twenty-one-year-old.

*Why do I really want to convert? I am not converting,* she reasoned, *I am choosing for the first time. I have not been baptized into any religion, so this is no conversion. That is a figment of someone else's imagination, someone who classifies everyone according to the religion of his or her parents. It doesn't really apply to me at all. I am simply choosing as a responsible person which religion I want to follow.*

*Why do I still want to become a Lutheran anyway? Hans is gone; I have had to look to others for companionship and love. I'm not really sure which of the young men I am really attracted to the most, but none of them seems to be a Lutheran. In fact, I haven't met any Lutheran fellows since Hans died. Maybe there aren't any. Do I really want to be a Lutheran, if there are no men to marry?*

Then the deeper meaning of her thoughts began to surface in her consciousness. *Was I becoming a Lutheran because I believed I should marry Hans, and am I now wondering about it simply because the men I have met all happen to be Mennonites? That is certainly not what Jesus taught. He was very clear that everyone is responsible for his or her own life and beliefs. Tina has made that clear in practically every lesson. That is also what my parents believe, even without saying so. I can see it in Mother's eyes every time we talk, that she is unhappy with the thought of my converting – there I go using that word again – from what they believe the Bible to be teaching.*

The women called to her to come and help them with a choice they were trying to make, and with that her thoughts returned immediately to the work before her. She went over cheerily to assist them with their purchases. When they had gone out of the store, she retraced her steps to finish what she was doing when they asked for her. Before she got to that part of the store, however, another figure darkened the doorway.

It was Heinrich Gerbrandt, whom she had met at the picnic. *Why should he be at the store in the middle of the day,* Leah wondered. She continued on her way to the area she was restocking, but noticed that Heinrich seemed a bit lost in the store. It was the first time she had noticed him come into the building, so that was understandable.

"Can I help you," she asked pleasantly, almost pleadingly.

"I am looking for something I can use as a bandage," he replied. "I cut my leg while we were working, and there was nothing to bind it up with at the site."

"We have some nice soft cloth over here," Leah led the way to where the bolts of cloth were stored and pulled out one that seemed suitable. "Would this be OK? How big a piece do you need?"

"The wound is right over my shin bone; I cut it with an axe. It slipped on some wet wood while I was chopping. Because the cut is straight up and down, it isn't bleeding very much, but if it isn't bound up, it will leave a gaping scar," he explained. "I tied a piece of rope over my trousers to keep it together while I walked over to the store."

"Would you like me to look at it and maybe bind it up for you?" she asked, looking deep into his dark eyes. He shrugged his shoulders and nodded.

"OK, can you roll up your pant leg for me, please?" she took charge. "I helped with some cuts and bruises my brothers got, so I sort of got some experience," she added, claiming a bit more knowledge than she really had, but meaning well by it.

Heinrich rolled up his pant leg, the gash where the axe had cut through wobbling back and forth as he worked the cloth into a roll at the knee. In the meantime, Leah cut a piece off the end of the bolt of linen and began to look for some healing salve they carried in their pharmaceutical section. She got a small dipper of water from the back of the store and looked around for somewhere to warm it. Seeing a candle nearby, she lit it in the fireplace at the back of the store, and held it under the bit of water in the dipper. When it was a bit warmer than room temperature, she dipped a piece of the clean cloth into it and wiped the area around the wound, to clean up the bit of blood and any dirt that might have gathered around the wound. She spread some of the balm on the cloth and placed it carefully over the wound, pulling the sides close together, and tying the cloth carefully behind Heinrich's leg. The pressure would prevent the wound from opening up, and allow it to heal with a minimum of scarring.

"Come back tomorrow, and I will check it for you," Leah told him, perhaps with a bit more authority than she wanted.

"I will probably go back to work tomorrow. I don't want to take time off, as I need the money badly," he replied, revealing his motives a bit too much for his own liking.

"Come when you are finished work, I'll wait for you here, and we can change your dressing then," Leah was insistent that Heinrich receive good treatment, but she really wanted to have him nearby, too. Her heart seemed to be doing strange things, now that she was so close to him and actually touching him. She hoped that he wouldn't notice the color in her cheeks or her trembling hands, but that he would think it was simply her exertion in binding the wound.

Heinrich was strangely stirred, too, by this lovely young woman whom he had met at the church picnic. They hadn't really had a chance to talk at all since then, but he had tried several times to get a glimpse of her, as he passed the store on his way to and from work.

"OK, I'll come tomorrow after work," he promised. "It certainly feels better, now that you have bound it up for me." He rolled his cut pant leg down over the bandage.

"Bring those pants on your way to work tomorrow, if you have some others you can wear, and lay them on the step of the store. I'll mend them for you while you are at work. We don't have many customers after lunch, so I'll have some time to put a patch into the cut for you," Leah found herself volunteering quite a bit on company time, but she felt it was what she should do, and Mr. Janzen wouldn't mind her doing a good deed for someone. He probably wouldn't guess her motives, anyway.

"Thank you," Heinrich replied, not quite knowing what to say, and certainly not knowing what to do with his flushed face. "Because my mother is also working in the Baron's laundry, there is no one at home to look after things like this. I'll be happy to bring you the pants, if you can fix them. I only have another old pair for work, so I will need these fixed somehow."

"Happy to help," she quipped triumphantly, knowing in her heart that she had netted her big fish. Heinrich left for the brick kiln, and Leah went back to stocking shelves.

As she reached for a bag to finish the area she was working on, Leah's thoughts returned to the musings that had occupied her, before she had overheard the Baron's wife telling about his thoughts on conversion.

*What do I really want? Am I really that much against what my parents have taught me, or was that just my juvenile rebellion getting the best of me? Was it just because I loved Hans and wanted to be like his people so much, that I began to look down on what I had been taught from childhood? Why am I saying 'was?' Have I changed? Am I really not so rebellious any more? Maybe I am growing up, and I'm more settled in what I want. Besides, Heinrich seems like a very dutiful Mennonite. I'll have to ask him whether he is a baptized church member. Maybe he's also trying to make up his mind, like I am.*

As her thought rolled on, she filled one shelf after another, until the place seemed more orderly than it had been in days. Mr. Janzen came around to tell her that it was time to go home, and then remarked that he was extremely pleased with how Leah had organized everything so neatly. Leah thanked him, got her coat and left for home. On the way home, she began to hum a melody that seemed to come from nowhere, and so she entered the house. Her mother looked up from her supper preparations to see what had come over her daughter, but was distracted by the insistent pleadings of one of the young boys.

# Chapter Seventeen

Father Daniel and Pastor Schmidt arrived at the von Ahlefeld mansion at the same time, and Menno arrived soon after, shuffling along on his crutches. Ben DeFehr representing the Calvinists, arrived at the same time. The Baron greeted each of them cordially, offered each a drink, and led them to the parlor, where he bade each take a comfortable chair. He showed Menno to the most comfortable chair, as he was the oldest of the men, and the most bowed by the ravages of age and hardship.

The parlor was furnished fairly simply, with a number of mismatched stuffed chairs, a table in the middle, and several smaller tables and cabinets around the walls. Cut flowers in a fine glass vase graced one small table between two windows, through which the warm summer sunshine streamed in patches on the great rug under their feet.

"Thank you for coming," began the Baron. "I have wanted to bring the four of you together for some time, but harvest, the building of the barns, and now the Mennonite Church, I haven't had the time. Besides, I wanted to wait until I had met with Duke Adolf of Holstein-Gottorp, to see whether we could make what I am going to propose to you all work. He wasn't too pleased with the idea, but when I told him that it would help to preserve peace on my estate, he finally agreed."

The men's curiosity was aroused. All eyes were now fixed on the Baron, who began easily, "As I mentioned, we have finished the harvest, and in spite of the rainy, late spring, we have had a reasonable return for our labor. The barns have been built, and the grain and hay have been stored properly under roof. The livestock is comfortable, and the calves and piglets, as well as lambs, chickens, geese, ducks, and colts are doing fine. These are the things that pertain to my estate; how have things gone with the private farms and businesses in your parishes?"

The clerics were astonished that the Baron would be asking them about their welfare. They looked at each other, as if to say, "You begin."

Father Daniel, as the one who had been there the longest, began. "My parish extends through all of the Baron's estate, so most of the people are his subjects. He has provided wonderfully for them, as usual. If it had not been for his getting seed barley, we would have had no crops this year, but the barley crop will sustain us quite adequately. Those who work in the shops of the Baron seem quite happy. I notice that, in each shop, there is a mixture of religions represented. That has provided some hefty discussions, I have heard."

The other men nodded their agreement. They were well aware, too, of the discussions between Catholics, Lutherans, Calvinists, and Mennonites. They had been put to the test themselves with the questions their parishioners had brought to them.

"My people have been especially blessed," added Menno. "So many have come to us over the past months, each with horror stories of persecution they have endured, and then we had the fever take so many in spring, including my Gertrude and my son David; we are a deeply hurting group, but God has been wonderful. Some things in our gardens have done very well, other things not so well, but generally, all is well. We have also profited from the Baron's largesse. He provided seed for us, as he did for everyone on his estate. We also have enough and to spare, for which we thank him and our Lord."

Ben DeFehr began rather hesitantly, "I am not the preacher, but I do represent those of our Calvinist faith that have been so graciously received here by the Baron. Ours has been a summer of terrible fear, flight in the incessant rain, and seemingly interminable sorrow. Only as we came to the Estate were we able to relax a bit. There were the difficulties of getting settled in as refugees, but thanks to the Baron and to so many of your parishioners," he paused, looking around at the others in the room, "we feel we have integrated fairly well into your community. God has ordained that we should be spared to serve Him."

"Yes, I can also attest to a good year," said Pastor Schmidt. "We are not many, and most of my parishioners are living in town. They are businessmen, and their businesses have gone reasonably well. Thanks to the Baron, we are doing quite well."

Each one was careful to give the Baron due credit for his assistance in a difficult time. Each had buried precious friends and loyal parishioners. They were well aware of the hurts that had nearly broken their community, and they were thankful that there seemed to be a new spirit of optimism and encouragement around.

"I was thinking that it would be a good thing for our entire estate community, if we had a Harvest Festival together – a sort of Thanksgiving Day. It would help to show our appreciation to our God for his goodness to us all, and it might help us learn to understand and appreciate each other more." The Baron was becoming quite animated, as he began to reveal more and more of what he had in mind.

"I would like your cooperation, if you would, to make this a completely satisfying event for us all," he continued. "It will mean getting your congregations together and preparing some things for the common group. We could set up tables in the town square, and I could see that the Kurhaus is open and available to all for the day; I will provide some musicians and some jugglers and clowns, and we could each bring some food items for a great common meal. That should give it quite an international flavour."

As the magnitude of the undertaking began to penetrate their minds, and the implications for ecumenical work, as well, the clerics sat in stunned silence. What did this mean for their particular beliefs? What would their parishioners, especially their elders, deacons, or other church authorities say?

"We could think of it mostly as a village festival," the Baron broke into their musings. "It wouldn't be entirely free of religious sentiments, though. I was thinking that we could have a combined prayer of thanksgiving to God, whom we all worship, though in different ways, and we could all enjoy some wholesome fun together as a community."

"We will have to take this up with our congregations," began Menno, tentatively. "We don't make all the decisions ourselves, like you politicians do." His attempt at humor was well received, and even the Baron laughed at this jab from the most pacifistic member of the group.

"There is one other thing that I thought might make this day special," continued the Baron, after they had all calmed down again. "I have heard that there may be those that are unhappy in their congregations, and I wondered whether we could bend the stipulations that have been given us by the Duke a bit, by clothing some things in other garments than they might appear on the surface."

Now he had everyone's attention. By now everyone knew that the Hildebrands wanted to convert to the Mennonite faith, and some knew that Heidi had intentions of converting to Lutheranism. Some others had also expressed dissatisfaction with their present church connections, so the topic of conversion was a moot theme in every conversation. Recent political directions seemed to indicate that there was a thaw in the icy relationships between Protestant princes and the Emperor, and that the Peace of Augsburg would hold. Nothing, however, had been said about converting from one religion to another. The assumption had been that everyone who desired a change had already made that new commitment. Nothing had been said, either, about young people in the Anabaptist groups who had not been baptized at all. They were considered heathen by the established Church, and they needed to convert to the True Religion, or perish eternally.

Diplomatically the Baron outlined what he had in mind for this great Thanksgiving Festival he had suggested. Menno and Pastor Schmidt nodded perceptively and agreed. Ben expected no one to convert to Calvinism among the Baron's subjects, so he remained quite neutral throughout the discussion. When it came to the Catholic priest, the Baron became much more diplomatic still, and approached his proposal in a slightly different manner from that with the Protestants. He suggested that there were probably couples with young babies to baptize, who would appreciate the opportunity to take care of that at such a grand occasion. At this, Father Daniel nodded. He, too, could see that this might work without too much backlash from his people, and the Bishop would not need to know all the details of what other groups did on that day. Yes, he could also agree to participate in the village festival.

• • •

Menno went back to the Menno Haus to finish a publishing job he was working on, but his mind churned over what the Baron had proposed. It seemed innocent enough, but it could also bring great trials to him and his congregation, particularly those who would become the main characters in the charade that was not a charade in the Thanksgiving Festival. Was it really duplicity? Would it really diffuse the animosity between the religious groups on the estate? Would he lose control over his flock?

"Hello, Menno," a voice came from the doorway. There stood Jake, on his way home from the shop.

"Why, Jake, I was just thinking about you," beamed Menno. That brought Jake to a sudden halt, for he could not imagine what Menno would be thinking about him. "Sit down there, please," he pointed to a chair, while he finished the last of what he was doing.

"The Baron called us preachers in this afternoon to talk about a plan he has for a big village festival of Thanksgiving, in which he wants all the churches to participate. There are some things about the Baron's plan that must be kept as secret as possible, but you are one who will be affected, so you must know. That means you will also be required to keep this from many people. Can I count on you?" Menno searched Jake's eyes for his reaction.

"Of course I can keep it a secret, I seldom talk anyway," Jake replied, somewhat coquettishly.

"You will be able to speak with Heidi, because she and her parents will also be involved, and you may tell your parents, because, in a way, they will also be affected. I will be speaking with Leah, as well, so she will know. These are the people from our group that are involved in the "plot", as I have come to call it," Menno continued.

"It's beginning to sound ominous," said Jake, rolling his eyes.

"In a sense it is ominous, but in another sense, it seems as though God is smiling on us in His benevolence. I believe we must be open to His surprises at any time, and this seems to be a time of surprise," Menno said, with a look of humorous glee in his tired, blue eyes.

"What are we to do then? What is it that I am supposed to know and keep secret?" Jake's curiosity had reached the ignition point, and he was ready to explode.

Menno came close to Jake and began to explain very softly what the leaders had decided. As Menno spoke, Jake's face broke into a smile, and then a wide grin. Menno, too, seemed to take some pleasure in what he was suggesting to Jake. They shook hands warmly, and Jake left for home in one direction, while Menno left in the other.

• • •

Pastor Schmidt reached his home with almost a bounding step to his walk. He greeted Mrs. Schmidt with extraordinary cordiality and then went straight to his office. He had much work to do. The Thanksgiving

Festival was only two weeks away, and he must prepare well for it. It would not do to have his church, which was admittedly one of the smallest in Bad Oldesloe, appear one whit behind the others in what it offered for the Festival. He must look over his membership list and see who could be made responsible for what. Were there any couples with a newborn that could be christened? Or couples that wanted to get married? Were there people who could create appropriate food items for a huge village-wide meal? *Oh my, there is just too much to do. How am I going to keep this secret from my wife and the others in his congregation, when I suddenly feel so unusually enthusiastic and animated?* Just then, he remembered that, only months before, they had lost their youngest son, and his spirit returned to its morose nest.

• • •

Ben DeFehr went to his colleagues in the cloth business, who were also his fellow Calvinists, and on the way he thought about what he would need to reveal, and what he should conceal, of the plan that he and the clerics, together with the Baron, had hatched.

"I met with the Baron this afternoon, and he would like to have a Thanksgiving Festival in two weeks, because of our harvest and the completion of his barns and the Mennonite church building, as well as our houses," he began. "Each religious group is supposed to be in charge of some of the activities, but the Baron will hire musicians, jugglers and clowns to brighten up the activities."

"What are we supposed to do? We are the smallest group, and we don't even have a proper church, like the others," wailed one of the men, "and our preacher is new here, so he won't have any idea of who can do what to help."

"Because we deal in cloth, he has asked us to provide bunting to brighten up the festival area, and to help decorate the town square with a harvest theme. We can ask the farmers for ideas and materials," replied Ben easily, trying to relieve the tension that had automatically come over the group as he had begun to explain what the meeting with the Baron was all about. "We could use some of the various solid color cloth roll ends and mix the colors in the bunting pieces. That would give a harvest effect."

The men began to see that this was not going to be so difficult, and it would show that they were grateful to the Baron for taking them in on the estate in their desperate need.

"We are also supposed to bring some food items for the great town meal that we will all have together. Each group is to bring something that represents their group, that is different from the local foods eaten by most of the people on the estate," added Ben. "The Baron will provide roasted pigs on a spit for everyone, but the other items must be provided by us all."

"Our women will think of something," replied another of the men, who took it all quite optimistically, and then added, "Flemings do well with fine things, so we should think of what kinds of fine pastries we can bring, for the others to sample."

"There is more to the day than this, but that will get us going for now," concluded Ben.

• • •

Father Daniel was not sure he completely understood what the Baron was driving at with this preposterous plan, but it did seem like a worthwhile thing to get the whole community together for Thanksgiving. As for the other items he had outlined, he was a bit perplexed as to how he would be able to uphold his end of the bargain. Being unmarried himself, he did not understand the implications of bringing food for that many people. Whom could he ask in his congregation? Probably Lizzy Hildebrand would be the obvious choice, but would she do that for him, or was her heart with those damned Mennonites? Heretics! A curse on them! Somehow he must find a way to make it look as though he was completely at ease doing things together with them.

Slowly he made his way to the manse, where his housekeeper had his supper nearly ready. He made it a practice to eat sparingly, but often, through the day, fitting his meals between his times of prayer and study. As he came in, he removed his outer robe and carefully hung it in a cabinet to the side of the hallway. He went to his study to think of a plan. It was difficult, when one had no one to talk things over with, he thought. His housekeeper was certainly not one with whom he could communicate anything important. She would have it as the theme of every gossip session in the whole country, and that within seeming minutes.

"Come for supper, Father," a voice drifted into his deep thoughts, and chased them far away. Wearily he rose, for he still suffered some weakness from the illness that had attacked him, and shuffled into the dining area.

"Why, Father, you look so tired," the housekeeper fussed, as she waited for him to seat himself.

"It must have been the activities of the day," he brushed off her concern.

The meal was eaten in silence, and when he was finished, Father Daniel excused himself and left the table. As the housekeeper went about the business of clearing the table and washing the dishes, he retired to his study, sat down in his comfortable chair, folded his hands before his face in deep contemplation and stared at the dying embers of his fireplace.

*What am I to do? Who will head up the catering for the whole community? Will Lizzy be willing to take this on? Will John and Lizzy, with Heidi, really leave my church, the one and only true Church? What will happen, if they do? Will others also choose to leave? Even if the Baron forbids them again, there may be some that will turn secretly, like the Hildebrands have. I'm not even sure of the Baron and his family; they seem like fickle water, now running this way, now running that way. Well, I must begin, so I will.*

# Chapter Eighteen

The day of the Thanksgiving Festival dawned bright and clear. A few clouds drifted over, appearing almost like pom poms helping the people celebrate. As the people came from all parts of the estate, people greeted one another gaily. Everyone seemed dressed up in their finest for the day. The women carried large baskets, conscripting sometimes unwilling sons to help carry heavy things.

The town square in Bad Oldesloe had never looked so inviting. Bright colored bunting hung from every tree, building and pole in the area. The centerpiece was a huge harvest display, with bundles of hay and grain tied with twisted strands of the same, garden vegetables, and assorted other things that had been harvested recently, or had been stored since last autumn. Large sacks of walnuts and hazelnuts attested to their ability to be stored for long times. They were joined by wooden crates of early varieties of apples, cherries and plums, as well as some dried prunes, apricots and apple slices, with green gooseberries, dark raisins and currants, both red and black, in colorful array in baskets, making a colorful and delectable-looking display. The Baron had also taken it upon himself to have some exotic fruits imported, which added to the international flair of the display. Jake had made a rustic backdrop for all of this.

Long tables had been arranged on sawhorses from the carpentry shop. Jake had seen to having all of this ready on time, and his crew set up all the tables and benches. When the baskets, dishes and platters of food arrived, there was ample place to put it on display. Everyone had been asked to bring trenchers and bowls, along with spoons and knives. Forks and ceramic plates were as yet unknown to North Europeans, besides God had created fingers for that purpose, and wooden trenchers served just as well.

An area had been set up with stones marking off fire pits, where the pigs were turned by sweating volunteers until they glowed golden brown in the heat above the embers. Other fire pits, with tripods for hanging pots, were devoted to those who needed to cook their wares before serving them.

The time had come for the Festival to begin, and the Baron, decked out in his best finery – striped bloomers over long grey stockings, a white blouse with ruffles down the front, and a short red waistcoat with gold trim. His hair was tied back with a colorful ribbon. His wife looked stunning in her silk dress, which she had gotten from the Calvinist cloth merchants. Their children looked equally stunning. Only their shyness prevented them from becoming the stars of the show.

"Hear ye, all ye people," shouted the Baron, trying to quiet the crowd, which took some time. He waited patiently until even those in the outer fringes of the crowd had stopped talking. "We are here today to celebrate and give thanks for what our good Lord has given us. We want to make it a time when everyone on the estate can be joyful together. Therefore, we have asked that each group – and this seems to be divided along religious lines – would participate in the activities according to the traditions that they have developed. Some things will be strange to you, because they have grown out of another tradition than your own, but please try to understand one another, regardless of whether you agree with what the other believes, or not."

A murmur went through the crowd, almost as if driven by a breeze. Then everyone's eyes focused once again on their nobleman.

"We will begin by eating together, so will Lizzy Hildebrand please come and explain how this will be done," the Baron stood there inviting Lizzy to come forward to his platform, so she could be heard. Reluctantly, Lizzy stepped forward and climbed the few steps to the platform. All eyes were now on her, and every tongue was quiet in anticipation of what it would taste in just a few moments.

Lizzy began to speak, but then she was asked to shout louder, so she began again, "Everyone has brought food along and put it on the long tables in the center of the square. You also have your own bowls, trenchers, cups and eating utensils. After you have picked up your piece of meat at the spit, you must begin on my left and proceed along either table, taking a bit from whichever dish you want, making sure that you leave some for the next person." At this there was a bit of giggling from the younger people, who knew she meant them by her remark. "I think there will be plenty for everyone, so eat heartily. Father Daniel, would you be so kind as to ask the Lord to bless this food?" The cleric moved to the platform and spreading his hands, he gave a short, meaningful prayer of thanksgiving for God's bounty, making special mention of the fear that the community had had early in the summer, that there would be no harvest at all to be thankful for. He also thanked God for the Baron and his family, who had made so much of this possible for everyone. A heartfelt 'Amen' sounded from everyone, as the prayer was concluded, then everyone began to move in the direction of the spits.

There were steaming bowls of bean and barley stew, boiled cabbage and carrots, leafy lettuce with oil and vinegar, with enough bread to feed an army. Lizzy's crew was kept busy cutting the shapeless loaves of white wheat bread, which had been baked in the large earthen oven close by the Baron's mansion. The Mennonite women had a pot of <u>Pluma Moos</u> going on one of the fires, and this proved to be one of the highlights of the day for everyone, the dried fruits tasting wonderful together in the sweet thickened pudding-like sauce. They were kept busy making more and more. The Calvinists' pastries, too, received accolades from everyone. How good they tasted with the Pluma Moos. The German roasted pig was more than appreciated by all.

A hush fell on the crowd, with hardly anyone venturing to speak with his neighbor, as mouthfuls of delicious food disappeared down hungry throats. The Baron took advantage of the lull in conversation to mount the platform again, "Ladies and gentlemen, there is more to our program. I have invited some special guests to come and entertain you; I will now call on them to come to the platform. Immediately jugglers and clowns came running in from a tent on the sidelines and began their act, alternating between feats of juggling and silly antics in strange costumes. Soon everyone was laughing heartily, or gasping in complete disbelief, as the troupe performed one antic after another, sometimes seeming to dare the very gravity that held them to the earth, and sometimes seeming to disappear in a cloud of imaginary obfuscation. When they had finished their performances, and the whole community cheered and clapped their approval, the Baron once more mounted the platform.

"Now, we have some parts of our program planned to take us away from the square. We will finish up here now and move to the things that are of special interest to each of you." At this, he listed the locations of the various other activities. These turned out to be special events in each of the churches represented. He made it clear that one did not have to be a member of a church, in order to attend any of these special festivities, but that many might be drawn to their own church for special reasons that would become evident, once they found out what was planned in each one.

"Then, tonight at eight o'clock, the Kurhaus will be open to everyone, either to attend the musical concert that I have arranged, or to use the warm mineral bath, naturally at my expense," he concluded with a bow. After another hearty cheer and much clapping by everyone, the women gathered their baskets and bowls with leftovers, and began to walk toward the church that they were attending.

Several couples made their way to the Catholic church for the christening of their babies. This had been arranged beforehand with them, and the church was appropriately decorated. Because of the Festival, many attended who could not always get there otherwise. Among them was a couple that no one recognized, for they had recently come to the estate as Anabaptist refugees. They were simply tired of running away, and had decided to return to the Catholic fold. Everyone was astounded at the new image of Mary that graced the old familiar spot. The Baron's seat was conspicuously empty, but his family sat in their accustomed seats.

In the Lutheran church there was a continuation of the festivities that had begun outside. There was also an infant baptism to be celebrated, and Pastor Schmidt did a commendable job of encouraging the parents and godparents to see that this tiny one was instructed in the way of the Lord. No one commented on the fact that Leah Derksen was not present: she had told Pastor Schmidt that she had a special reason to attend the dedication service at the Mennonite church.

The Calvinists had no special event to celebrate, and no church to celebrate in, but they were deeply thankful for their safety and the Baron's welcome on the estate, so there were many prayers of thanksgiving rendered with deeply-felt gratitude to a holy and sovereign God. Not forgotten was the extra income that the festival had brought to them in the sale of bunting and silk.

This was to be the dedication of the Mennonite church building, so every Mennonite on the estate, plus a number of visitors, including Mennonite bishops from other areas in northern Europe, and the Baron himself, were present. Since the festivities had been in Bad Oldesloe and the church was in Wuestenfelde, the Baron had arranged for wagons to transport older people and mothers with infants to their destination. The rest walked in groups, chatting merrily along the way. As soon as the group was assembled, Menno stood up with the help of his crutches, and addressed the congregation. Everyone had wondered why there were some benches at the front that were roped off, so that no one could sit on them.

"We have gone through many trials, but God has been faithful to us and given us a Promised Land," he began, his soft voice barely audible above the rustle on the benches. The quietness of his voice brought a greater hush to the group. This was the first time most had been in the new sanctuary, so the things that could be seen were carefully evaluated for their workmanship and utility. People noticed the carefully turned tops on the backs of the benches – yes, backs – Jake had taken these on as a special project in the shop, and now people were sitting comfortably on wooden pews with backs, and with turned tops at the ends, no less. The artwork seemed to blend in so well with the purpose and the spirit of thankfulness, that no one seemed to object to having something looking better than absolutely plain in their new church. The front of the church was simple, but nicely done in plaster and wood, making a lovely effect. The windows were tall and slender, without special decoration. No stained glass here, as in cathedrals throughout Europe. Everything spoke of a simple faith, ready to sacrifice all for the Lord, who had given His all for them.

A Vorsänger announced a hymn, and intoned it. Soon everyone joined in heartily.

"As part of the dedication of our new building, we want to hear something from our visiting guests," continued Menno, and called first on the Baron. He rose, conspicuous in his fancy clothes, came to the front, and addressed the crowd.

"This building represents something that most people thought impossible. A people who have suffered unheard-of persecutions in various homelands has come together on Fresenburg Estate, has proven beyond a doubt that they are industrious, honest, moral, and believing people. God has shown me and everyone else on the estate, that Mennonites are true worshippers of Jesus Christ, and He has put it into the hearts of Menno and his followers here to build this sanctuary in His honor, so that the gospel of Jesus Christ may go forth to young and old. I am proud of what the Mennonites have accomplished on my estate. I believe God is happy with what He sees here today. May God richly bless you all."

Menno had to sit down for the Baron's address, and now he rose and thanked the Baron for his generosity and his goodwill toward the Mennonites. He then called on one after another of the Bishops to give greetings. Some spoke quite long, others not too long; all spoke riddles, the younger folk thought. The enthusiasts among them thought that some could have given their speech more gusto, and those who thought all spiritual words must be solemn felt blessed by the very ones that others thought were too dry and dusty. At length – again, to some, at long, long length – the greetings were finished, and Menno got up to announce further proceedings.

"We have some joyous things to perform this day," he began, "and it gives me great pleasure to have these take place as part of our dedication of the building. It somehow gives me hope for the future, as we now proceed with the next thing on our agenda. Would those who have talked with me about receiving believers baptism please come forward."

The congregation gasped. They knew of no baptism. Eyes began wandering to the rear of the room, where there seemed to be a bustle. With every eye straining to see who would appear, the place once again became still as a morgue. First, the deacons and their wives came forward and stood behind Menno on the platform. Jacob and Eva were among them. Then, to everyone's surprise, in walked Jake and Leah Derksen, Heidi Hildebrand with her parents, and Heinrich Gerbrandt. As the group lined up in front of the church, everyone's eyes fell on the two lovely ladies standing before them. Both were stunning in their new dresses and carefully done hair. The men, too, looked impressive in their new suits. Even John Hildebrand had bathed to take away the hog barn smell, and changed into the finest clothes he could find, and Lizzy, too, had changed from what she had worn to the festival.

Menno led in the baptism ceremony, asking each candidate some pointed questions about the genuineness of their faith, which each one answered with dignity and clarity. Each in turn knelt before Menno to receive the pouring of water on their head in the name of the Father, the Son and the Holy Spirit. Then the group was welcomed into the Mennonite Church by the deacons, including Jacob and Eva. These hugged their children especially tightly, as their eyes clouded over.

"This is not the end of our celebrations today," continued Menno. These young people have now openly declared their faith in the Lord Jesus Christ, but they also wish to declare their love for one another. We will now proceed to the weddings of the two couples before us." At this he assembled the couples before him, with parents standing appropriately beside their children. For Jacob and Eva, this meant standing in the middle between Jake and Leah, which they did with obvious joy. The Hildebrands stood on the outside by Heidi, and the Gerbrandts came forward and stood on the outside by Heinrich.

Menno proceeded with the wedding ceremony, announcing that each of the couples had already been to the town hall for the legal proceedings, and that this was the spiritual union that would be blessed by the Lord. He then asked each couple to repeat vows that would bind them in faithfulness to each other. Each one answered "I do" at the proper time, and then Menno pronounced them man and wife. At this, an almost inexpressible joy flooded the building, exploding in a joyous whispering as the couples made their way to the rear of the building and outside. A few boisterous ones even clapped their hands. The newly-received Mennonites formed a receiving line where they were greeted heartily by one and all. The newly-married couples were greeted especially heartily and wished God's richest blessings in their marriage. Jacob and Eva, John and Lizzy, and the Gerbrandts beamed profusely over their children, who were now stepping out on their own.

It took a long time for the crowd to pull themselves away from the friendly and joyous occasion, and from the new building they had come to dedicate. Eventually, the older ones began to depart, again taking advantage of the Baron's wagons that waited for them. Then families with little ones felt they needed to leave, and last of all, Menno and the two couples were left standing in front of the church building.

"This has been a marvelous day," exclaimed Heidi, beaming at Jake, then at Menno.

"Yes, I agree," said Leah, starry eyes fixed on Heinrich.

"I believe we will need something to eat, before we go to the Kurhaus for the concert," said Jake, looking furtively at Menno. The kindly gentleman pretended not to have heard him and changed the subject.

"It will be good to have you young folks as part of our congregation," he ventured, "but I know that for you, Jake and Heidi, it will mean being in Lübeck for the next year, while each of you finishes your training."

"Yes, we leave tomorrow," said Jake with a wry twist to his mouth.

"Leah and I will be away from work for a couple of days, but will remain in Bad Oldesloe," said Heinrich, "both of us want to continue our work here."

• • •

Father Daniel had played along with the ruse, knowing that there was no way he could prevent those who wished to convert from doing so, no matter what the consequences. All of the Mennonites on the estate had run for their lives from the church and its magistrates. They had survived, in spite of the sword, the fire, or the rack. The Inquisition had not helped one bit to stifle this drain on the church. Instead, the conversions seemed to be increasing in frequency, as more people seemed to see in the traditional faith a weakness that turned them elsewhere. *What was it that this accursed monk in Wittenberg had said? "The just shall live by his faith," I believe it was. Somewhere in Romans, he said, but a quotation from somewhere in the Old Testament: Habakkuk 2:4, I believe he said. I don't know why his Abbot allowed him to read the Bible for himself, anyway. It's dangerous! Downright dangerous it is, to read the Bible without direction from the church. When Menno started reading the Bible for himself – a priest reading the Bible for himself, instead of following* the church liturgy and readings – he found that the Bible didn't seem to agree with the church's teachings. How could that possibly be? The church has preserved the scriptures all these sixteen centuries, and he says that the church doesn't know what the Bible teaches. He frowns on tradition, he says, because it teaches for doctrines the commandments of men. Jesus said that about the Pharisees, but surely He can't mean us. Or can He? Dangerous or not, perhaps I should get a copy of the Bible for myself and check. Now, should I get a German Bible, one that Luther translated, or stick with our old Latin one? Safer to stick with Latin for the moment, avoids suspicion, I guess. That's what these other men read, anyway, but not everyone can do so. Perhaps I'll learn where these damned heretics learned their false beliefs.

Yes, there were two babies to christen today, and there was even an older couple from among the immigrants that sought baptism for the third time after having gone over to the Mennonites, but everyone knows now that the Hildebrands jumped over to the Mennonites. I must admit, though, that Lizzy played her part wonderfully. No one suspected her of being a traitor to the faith, as she single-handedly organized the whole food distribution and eating this noon. Menno's getting a valuable worker there.

His thoughts continued: And, when it came to our own congregation, Lizzy whipped them into shape, as only she could. The women made all sorts of traditional items from this area, and the men found the best wines and beers to bring out for the meal. Then, Lizzy seemed to disappear into thin air. I suspect she went over to the Mennonite church building dedication, what with her sympathies in that direction. They wouldn't have also had a baptism today, would they?

And, to think that a ruse was used to allow Heidi to be married to that Derksen fellow. Brother to a criminal, no less. Destroyer of church property, and the Holy Virgin at that. I'm certainly glad that the Baron only allowed conversions on this one day, or I wonder who would be the next to jump to the Mennonites. I have to admit, though, that the rest of the Derksen family seems to be quite respectable, and Jake will make a good husband for Heidi.

Probably all for the taste of that – what did they call it again – Pluma Moos, I believe. I must admit, though, that their Pluma Moos was delicious.

*I wonder if there was any left over. I'll get ready now and go to the concert at the Kurhaus. If there was some left, then they would have brought it there, I would think.*

• • •

Pastor and Mrs. Schmidt were eating a light meal, before going out to the Kurhaus for the evening concert. It had been a hectic day, but overall, a very good day. The Festival had gone exceptionally well. It seemed that every part of it went off as planned, and with great interest on the part of the whole community. Dividing the groups by religious backgrounds proved both necessary and beneficial, as it allowed each group to introduce itself in a somewhat non-threatening way to the others. Food is pretty democratic, after all. Pastor Schmidt's thoughts began to trace through the day.

*Our* Leberwurst *and* Sauerkraut, *served with* Mischbrot, *seemed to go over very well with many people. There always seemed to be a line-up at our stall. My wife is such a champion; she practically managed it by herself. The other women seemed to find it beneath their dignity to stand behind a seething kettle and dish up slimy* Leberwurst *sausage. They didn't seem to mind going over to the Calvinists for their dainties or the Mennonites for their* Pluma Moos, *though.*

As they finished their meal of bread and sliced sausage and cheese, washed down with some wine and mineral water, the Schmidts began to think it about time to make their way over to the Kurhaus for the evening concert. It would be good to relax and enjoy an evening of entertainment in a lovely setting.

• • •

Ben DeFehr and the other Calvinists went to the DeFehr house to discuss the day. They had to admit that the ruse had worked wonderfully, at least for the moment, in making it possible for those who wanted to convert to another religion to be able to do so without recrimination. Some of the men reported talking with Catholics that seemed to show an interest in their religion; that was a good beginning. Such people would hardly be ones to have to fear in the future. Their dainties had interested almost everyone, so that part of their day's contribution had been an unqualified success. The buntings, too, had provided color and verve to the square, giving everyone a festive spirit. All in all, they felt their day had been quite good for their group, especially in the complexity of life in the context of the estate. Besides, sales of cloth had trebled in the past weeks, giving them a handsome profit. For this, too, they were deeply thankful.

● ● ●

Jacob and Eva's house was a beehive of activity. Jake and Heidi, as well as Heinrich and Leah, together with the Hildebrands and the Gerbrandts, were all there for supper. The women got busy setting out the dishes, cutting bread, sausage and cheese for the evening meal, while the men sat in the other room, teasing the young bridegrooms mercilessly about what they had gotten themselves into. They, in turn, teased their elders about incidents in their family's past that had provided their share of mirth. The younger children were mostly draped over bench-beds, hardly able to keep their eyes open.

"All's ready," called Leah from the family room. The men, like eager puppies, filed through the doorway to see the table ready for their multiple-family meal. Each found a place near his mate, and Jacob signalled that he would say grace. All heads bowed, as he recited,

"God is great, God is good, Let us thank Him for this food, Amen."

"Amen," chorused the rest of the group. No one seemed to need prodding to dig in. The children each received a trencher of food from Eva and were told to find a seat away from the table, while the young couples were allowed to choose first from everything.

The young women radiated a quiet beauty that permeated everything in the room. Their young husbands couldn't take their eyes off of their new wives. The parents couldn't keep their eyes off their suddenly-matured daughters, thinking of the little girls that they had been such a short time ago.

"Where will you go for your wedding week?" asked Jacob, looking at Leah and Heinrich. The blushing bride looked at her husband and nodded for him to speak. Heinrich, not being a man of many words, couldn't think of what to say. Everyone waited while he collected his thoughts. Finally, he managed to find some words.

"We aren't going far, or for many days. First of all, we both want to be at work as soon as possible, and secondly, we haven't got money to go for a long time. Because both of us started work a relatively short time ago, we have had to use quite a lot of our savings – and quite a bit from our parents – to get our place ready to move into. We'll just stay here in Bad Oldesloe, in our new home, which is a nice apartment in one of the new buildings that Jacob – I mean, Father – built recently."

"And where will you stay tonight, before you take off for Lübeck tomorrow?" asked Eva, looking at Heidi and Jake.

"Well, actually the Baron has asked us to come to his mansion. He has made a room available for us, complete with maid," said Heidi teasingly.

"Oh, go on. He would never condescend to allow us commoners to sleep in his place," responded Leah. "You're joking."

"Why, what would make you think so?" asked Heidi, as innocently as she could possibly say it.

"Come on, tell us where you will be. We'll miss you soon enough, since you have to leave tomorrow morning for Lübeck. I'm so glad you're going to be staying with Olga, while you continue your studies and your apprenticeship. It somehow makes me feel good and secure," Eva couldn't help but already be feeling the loss of her first daughter and greatest helper.

"Well, actually, we'll be staying at the Gasthaus in Bad Oldesloe, right across from the Kurhaus, where we want to spend the evening," said Jake, matter-of-factly. "The coach will leave from the Gasthaus right after breakfast, so that we can make it to Lübeck in one day. We need to hurry now, though, so that we'll get to the concert on time. We couples plan to bathe in the mineral waters of the Kurhaus after the concert, so we have packed some appropriate clothes and towels for that."

"I guess I can't tell you to behave yourselves on your wedding night," joked John. "Perhaps we should all go to the Kurhaus tonight. It would be a good way to relax and enjoy the day a bit longer."

Jacob and Eva looked at one another furtively.

"I'm old enough to look after Aron and Frederic," piped Sarah. Her parents looked at each other again, this time with a bit of surprise in their eyes. Was their younger daughter really that grown up already? The Hildebrands and the Gerbrandts seemed to indicate that it would be a good plan, too.

"All right," said Jacob sternly, "but there won't be any dancing on my part. I just won't do such a thing." Everyone smiled and nodded, then got up from the table and began preparations for the walk over to the Kurhaus.

• • •

The atmosphere in the Kurhaus was electric. Those who considered themselves the upper echelons of society could be seen, preened and coiffed to the Nth degree, making sure to drift from one circle to the next, to be seen by all, and discussing major issues of world import, or niceties of no import at all. Common town folk gathered in another area together, discussing the events of the day and the respective merits of one dish or another they had tasted that noon. The Mennonites, including the new ones, stayed in a small group in the back, looking at first one group, then another, in utter astonishment. On the one hand, they felt ashamed by their plain appearance in the company of those who were so ostentatious, and on the other hand, they prided themselves in reflecting the glory of the Lord in their simplicity.

The Hildebrands had been part of the town folk before, and were known to all of them. Now they were shunned by their former friends, who had heard by this time that they had become Mennonites. The Derksens were also known to everyone, but were not spoken to, lest the town folk or the society folk should be thought to have inclinations to convert. The Gerbrandts, being newer, were just seen as baggage with the other two families.

All eyes, though, fell on the two young couples, stunning in their special clothing and well-groomed hair. They appeared almost as though they had recently been married. No one except the Mennonites guessed that they were, in fact, newlyweds of that day.

A hush came over the room, as the keeper of the Kurhaus announced the arrival of the Baron and his wife. The crowd moved to their seats, standing as a fanfare from the orchestra announced their entrance into the festive hall. Helping his wife into her chair, the Baron stood and faced the crowd.

"Welcome, one and all, to this town festival, and especially, to this concert in the Kurhaus. As I promised, there will be no charge for tonight's program; I have taken care of that. Nor will there be a charge for moderate amounts of drink you might wish to receive in the intermission. Now, would Jake and Heidi Derksen and Heinrich and Leah Gerbrandt please step forward."

Neither couple knew what the Baron had in mind, but they felt that, in spite of their blushing and insecurity, they had better obey the Baron's wish. With a bit of fussing with hair and ribbons, they managed to find their way to the front, where the Baron stood. He bade them come beside him, one couple on each side.

"As you all know, we have an edict on the estate – indeed in the whole realm of Adolf, Duke of Holstein-Gottorp – that no one is allowed to convert from one religion to another. This has produced occasional tension on the estate, as you all know. It became especially strained, when the Hildebrand family indicated their desire to convert to the Mennonites. I decided, and the Duke agreed, to approach the religious leaders of our town, to see whether a one-day moratorium could be declared, in which anyone could convert, if they so wished. Joshua proclaimed it this way: "<u>Choose you this day</u> whom ye will serve." As it turned out, the Hildebrands, including their daughter Heidi, did decide to convert to the Mennonites, and they were baptized during the dedication of their new building today. Leah Derksen, on the other hand, decided not to convert to the Lutherans, but to join with her family in the Mennonite church, so she, too, was baptized along with her brother Jake and another young man named Heinrich Gerbrandt. All of these came from Mennonite families, so there was no conversion involved. Their having been baptized into the Mennonite church, however, opened another possibility – that of marriage within their church. They do not recognize the state wedding as spiritually binding, so they perform another ceremony, just as our other churches do, and Heinrich and Leah, as well as Jake and Heidi, were married at the dedication service this afternoon, too. It gives me great pleasure to introduce to you Mr. and Mrs. Jacob Derksen Jr and Mr. and Mrs. Heinrich Gerbrandt."

With that, everyone stood to honor the young couples, who stood blushing before them. A march was then called for, and the Baron and his wife led the way, beckoning the young couples to follow, as they stepped gaily to the pumping music. Bewildered, but motivated by the Baron's generous introduction, they followed the example of their lord, and soon almost everyone in the room was marching around the Kurhaus festive hall to the lively music of the orchestra. When the piece stopped, everyone sat down, and the orchestra began a slow medita-tive piece that calmed everyone's spirit. Alternating the style of pieces throughout the night, the orchestra played one style of dance after another, intermingled with pieces that showed off one instrumentalist's talents or another's.

At intermission, the lines formed to receive drinks from the bar that the Baron had arranged along one side of the hall. Soon everyone was gathered around the newlyweds and their parents, congratulating them and wishing them well. They were asked what they planned to do, and both couples could respond with assurance that their plans were working out well. The parents beamed in the background and fielded questions from their neighbors, bringing them into the conversation. The Derksens and the Gerbrandts were Mennonites when they arrived on the estate, so no one asked them about their beliefs. The Hildebrands, on the other hand, were the converts, and all kinds of questions were leveled at them, to which they were able to reply with candor and grace, as Menno had taught them. Father Daniel and Pastor Schmidt stood together in one corner, observing the crowd gathered around the Mennonites, and shook their heads in wonder. Then, they looked at each other, and Pastor Schmidt winked at his fellow cleric, saying, "I guess, if we as opposite poles can stand and talk to each other, the folks can talk to those of other faiths, too." The priest agreed, and both joined the group congratulating the couples.